Dig Your Job

Keep it or Find a New One
The Not-So-Serious Career Handbook

G.L. Hoffman

Copyright © 2008 by G.L. Hoffman

Published by JobDig, Inc.
10300 Valley View Road | Suite 101 | Eden Prairie, MN 55344
www.jobdig.com | Toll Free Phone: 877.456.2344 | Email: digyourjob@jobdig.com

All rights reserved. No part of this book may be reproduced in any form or by any means without written permission from the author or publisher.

Design by Brenda Anderson

ISBN: 978-0-578-00458-7

"It's all in here! G.L. Hoffman's *DIG YOUR JOB* is full
of answers to your most pressing job questions."
– *Marshall Goldsmith, NYT and WSJ #1 best-selling author of What Got You Here
Won't Get You There: How Successful People Become Even More Successful*

"G.L. is the perfect Dutch Uncle to everyone who knows him. I'm glad this serial entrepreneur has finally put his knowledge about job hunting and careers in writing. His book packs so many useful insights that anyone is guaranteed to walk away with ideas they can put to use immediately. What's most valuable about it is the way the book will make you THINK. It will stimulate you to bend and shape the ideas presented so they'll work for YOU."
– *Nick Corcodilos, www.AskTheHeadhunter.com*

"I'm astounded by the amount of information in this book. I can see referring back to this over years; I can see printing out pages to talk over with people when addressing a problem. It's a terrific resource for small business people and for people in the workforce."
– *Becky McCray, Consultant to Small Towns, Small Businesses,
www.SmallBizSurvival.com*

"The perspective of this book alone would make it special, because no one else seems to look at jobs with such practical, I-can-use-this-today types of tips. G.L.'s writing style makes the reading so comfortable, like a conversation in your living room, that it takes reflection to realize that most of these insights can actually turn your life around. Don't be deceived by the comfortable clarity of this book. It has depth!"
– *Conrad Hake of Conolay Consulting, Inc.*

"G.L. is a walking, talking (and now writing) testament to success through positive action. He is one of my heroes. He has done you a great service by putting his terrific tips and ideas down into this easy to read book...so you too can apply them and become (more) successful."
– *Simon Foster, founder of SimonDelivers and principal, Spencer Stuart*

After years of waiting, I think we have finally found the most definitive career advice book since Dick Bolles first published his Parachute series. *DIG YOUR JOB* is aptly suited for the current generation of those either working or hoping to start working with a wealth of practical, oftentimes humorous, no-nonsense advice that virtually everyone can truly relate to and benefit from. Dig Your Job is an absolute must-read for anyone who works or is looking for work."
– *Toby Dayton, author of the blog Diggings*

"...Another good one is "Please Don't Come to My Workplace, Mommy," where he gives us a list of five things we should tell our parents about what not to do. Really hilarious, but I emailed my mom as a preemptive measure just in case she got any funny ideas about being in my office's neighborhood."

– www.playboy.com

"*DIG YOUR JOB* is jam packed with practical tips that you can put to use TODAY to be noticed, appreciated and successful on the job. If you want to be one of the best, get the book and live it!"

– Drew McLellan, www.DrewsMarketingMinute.com

"Had G.L. Hoffman's book *DIG YOUR JOB* had been published earlier in my career it would have saved me countless mistakes."

– Gary Cohen, author of *Just Ask!*, principal of CO2 Partners

"*DIG YOUR JOB* packs in more than two hundred quick-read, mini-lessons from someone who has built a bunch of companies and understands jobs. Reading this book is a short time investment that will make a long-term difference in your career."

– Penelope Trunk, www.BrazenCareerist.com

"Finally, a practical guide that tells it like it is, for those of us in the real world. Whether you are job hunting or hoping for a promotion, don't leave home without this book!"

– Candice Broom, editor www.MomMostTraveled.com

"I am not a voracious reader of books, which may say something about my intellectual curiosity, on the other hand I prefer to rationalize it by saying that I am too busy and have a short attention span anyway. In any case, this is just one of the reasons I love the way G.L. writes and especially like what he has done with this book. Words of one syllable, to the point, delivered with good humor and each entry filled with "learnings" that would be helpful at any stage of one's career."

– Dave Opton, founder & CEO ExecuNet

"*DIG YOUR JOB* is an excellent resource for both people who are new to the workforce and for seasoned professionals. Not only does the book provide the reader with a myriad of job hunting tips, but also advice about how to advance your career by being the best possible employee."

– Sharon Reed Abboud, author of *All Moms Work: Short-Term Career Strategies for Long-Range Success*

"*DIG YOUR JOB* condenses all that 'Dad Advice' we received from our fathers, but probably never really heard and processed until we were adults, in one amazingly inspirational resource."
– *Christopher Buttner, President, PRRThatRocks.com*

"*DIG YOUR JOB* is the "owner's manual" every college graduate should receive along with their diploma. G.L. Hoffman has created a career management roadmap filled with insightful tips for landing and keeping a job and maintaining your sanity along the way. "
– *Barbara Safani of Career Solvers*

"In my career as an HR exec and then a business manager, I have interviewed and counseled hundreds of young people. Most could benefit greatly from reading and rereading this book."
– *Jeannette Rupert, Wells Fargo Bank*

"G.L. Hoffman has packed *DIG YOUR JOB* with simple (but not easy) tips on how you can love the job you have, and get a new one if you hate the one you have. Packed with 200+ tips that you can use RIGHT NOW, this is a must have book for anyone wanting to improve their job. Can you dig it?"
– *Phil Gerbyshak, www.slackermanager.com and author of 10 Ways to Make It Great!*

"*DIG YOUR JOB* is like having a mentor in a box. Hoffman picks up where schools leave off. He offers hundreds of ideas to ease the transition into the workforce and make those first few jobs as successful as possible."
– *Randy Street, author of the NYT best selling book Who: The A Method for Hiring*

"G.L. Hoffman offers the kind of career advice I respect: equal parts of tough love and understanding, with plenty of thoughtful insight to go around. This is more than a career guidebook, it's a career mind-set. If you want greater professional success in today's workplace, then you don't just want to read this book - you need to read this book."
- *J.T. O'Donnell, nationally syndicated advice columnist and author of CAREEREALISM: The Smart Approach to a Satisfying Career*

"Just like I like it: No candy-coating. No band-aid therapy. Simple, authentic, words-of-wisdom that are timeless and timely. Stuff our Dads, and other folks we respect and admire, have served up to us with and without our asking…which are all DEAD-ON. Period end of sentence."
– *Kimberlie Dykeman, TV host and producer, international spokesperson, motivational speaker and author of Pure Soapbox*

"This book is chock full of helpful career nuggets that any member of Gen Y will find instructive and inspiring." – *Ben Casnocha, author of My Start-Up Life: What a (Very) Young CEO Learned on His Journey Through Silicon Valley*

"Reading this book is like sitting down with a business executive over some barbecue and hearing his most sage advice and insights about carving out a successful career. While G.L. Hoffman can be very funny and informal, his wicked intelligence about work deserves your total seriousness."
– *Liz Wolgemuth, Reporter, Money & Business , U.S. News & World Report*

"*DIG YOUR JOB* provides shovels-full of great career advice, especially for those dealing with today's tough job market." – *Peter Weddle, CEO, WEDDLE's LLC*

"Do you truly dig your job? If not, G.L. Hoffman has more than 200 practical and entertaining tips to help you improve your current gig or find one that you'll dig more. He has even included Recession Protector Tips for thriving in tough economic times."
– *Pamela Skillings, career coach, author of Escape from Corporate America: A Practical Guide to Creating the Career of Your Dreams, www.escapefromcorporate.com*

"I read a tremendous amount of books and there are precious few that I am willing to put my name behind. This book easily makes my top ten for recommendations. This book is all about real world information that helps people not only be job ready, but stay job ready. G.L. does a masterful job of whizzing you through 200 plus quick take tips that contain a lifetime of wisdom."
– *Nick Reddin, World of Work Solutions, Manpower*

I wish I'd had G.L. Hoffman's *DIG YOUR JOB* when I left the comfort of school for my first job and struggled to understand the harsh realities of the working world. His wise advice and practical how-to tips would've saved me from making career blunders in my youth many years ago – and it will definitely do the same for today's young workers just beginning their careers. But it goes beyond being a helpful guide for new employees. As a Baby Boomer who has been working for longer than I care to remember, I was very impressed with G.L.'s insights and recommendations, and learned several strategies that I know will help me to continue advancing in my career. I particularly enjoyed reading about "The Art of Getting Ahead," and as a Boomer, I got a big kick out of "How Gen Y Can Handle the Baby Boomers at Work." Hilarious (and so true)! Wrapping up his book with a chapter sharing career advice (good and bad) from many dads was the icing on the cake. Anyone interested in having a successful career should dig into *DIG YOUR JOB!*
– *Bonnie Lowe, www.Best-Interview-Strategies.com*

"Loved *DIG YOUR JOB!* From an entrepreneur's and boss' point of view, the job advice is rock solid. All things we bosses are always looking for and wish everyone knew how to do… lots of common sense that is sadly uncommon today. G.L.'s advice is right on and I will be reading it with my five and seven year old daughters! Last but not least the company building lessons cover the ups and downs of my last 11 years building LatPro.com perfectly, a great read with a very authentic and trustworthy voice."

– Eric Shannon, President, LatPro, Inc.

"As a college senior, *DIG YOUR JOB*. Keep it or Find a New One by G.L. Hoffman, has taught me invaluable lessons that I will be able use time and time again as I make the transition from student to employee. It is full of insightful, relative, yet comedic and unpretentious suggestions on how a twenty something like me can actively become a part of the workforce even in a time of economic hardship. Previous to reading this book, someone would tell me every day that I was not going to get a job in my field. Now, armed with the tips I learned from Hoffman's book, I'm confident that it is up to me to make things happen, and that they will."

– Leah Metz, senior at the University of St. Thomas, 2009

"Whether just starting your career or looking to put some life back into your professional journey, *DIG YOUR JOB* delivers solid and powerful lessons in a format that is quick and easy to digest for everyone. With a range of hot ideas geared toward any level of employment that includes interview tips, how to inject a new passion into your job or even smart advice on insulating your employment from the impact of a recession… I'd call the decision to add this book to anyone's personal library a no-brainer. This is the new career bible for today's careerist."

– Chris Hoyt, RecruiterGuy, www.RecruiterGuy.net

"G.L. Hoffman's book supplies volumes of practical advice without ever losing sight of the big picture: create meaning and engagement in your work, and you'll build a truly successful career for yourself. But there is more to *DIG YOUR JOB* than just career advice. What you get here is a book jam-packed with much needed wisdom that could be applied to just about any other area of your life. "Don't blame others," "Worry is the misuse of your imagination," "Change your attitude" - G.L. doesn't mince words in making it clear: no one but you is responsible for your happiness, whether at work or in life. Following G.L.'s advice will not just make you better at crafting a career of your dreams: it will help you build a better life."

– Izabella Tabarovsky, www.ProjectCreativeVision.com:
Purposeful Career Coaching for Those Seeking to Make a Life, Not Just a Living

Table of Contents

Foreword 1

Introduction 2

Ch 1: On the job improvement tips 3

Ten New Year's Resolutions... 4
Be a Job Improver Instead of... 5
What To Do When The Boss... 6
How to Be Excellent in Meetings 7
Your First Big Presentation 8
Keep Learning to Get Ahead 8
Work is Not Just an 8-5 Thing 9
Telling Time or Building Clocks 9
How To Handle the Negative... 10
Are You Anonymous at Work? 11
How To Handle Negative... 12
Get Engaged At Your Job 13
The Art of Getting Ahead 14
Wrong Job or Just Bored? 15
Do You Have a Clap... 16
Small Companies are Better 16
They Yelled at Me... 17
I Want To Quit After Only... 17
How To Cope With Criticism... 18
Plussing 18
Employers Must Earn... 19
Recognize and Fix... 20
How Gen Y Can Handle... 21
Little Overlooked Things... 22

Five Things To Do At Work... 23
Who is Your Real Boss 24
Five Must-Do Things... 25
Should I Settle At My Job... 26
What's the Trick...Management 27
What Bosses Like 28
Making Your Bones 29
Advice You Won't Hear... 30
Good Luck...Lone Ranger 31
Making Chicken Salad... 32

Chapter 2: Preparing for a new job 33

Interview...Job You Don't Want 34
How To Find Your True... 34
You Don't Get In... 35
Ask Others About Their Careers 35
Five Things To Look For... 36
Urgency in Your Job Seeking 36
College Grads...the Summer Off 37
Five Things To Do Now... 38
I Just Graduated and... 39
Resume Liars 39
Specificity Sells...Cover Letters 40
Job Seekers Should Know... 40
Use a Strong Headline... 41
Brutal But Honest... 42
Are You on a Career Path? 44
Five Things You Can Do Now... 45
Please Don't Come... 46

Ch 3: How to master the interview 47

Two Counter-Intuitive... 48
Before the Interview... 48
How To Start the Job Interview 49
When Can You Start? 51
The Winning Job Interview 52
Body Language... 53
Three Types of Interview... 54
Four Gutsy Things To Say... 55
What To Say... 55
It's Not the Job, Stupid... 56
Three Job Candidates... 57
The "When Can You Start?... 59
How to Un-Bore Yourself 60
Eats, Shoots & Leaves... 61
The Interview is Over, Not 62
The Class Everyone Thought... 62
Yogi Berra, JobSeeker 64

Ch 4: Attitude determines altitude 65

Standard Responses... 66
Lessons from Famous Movies... 67
The YeahButs Have Arrived 67
How To Walk Your Talk 68
Learn from your Mistakes 68
Taking a Step Back 69
Learn to be an Innovator 70
Money Saving Tips 70
Simple Things 71
Get Happy For Others 71
Beware of People... 72
Role Models Needed 72
I Work in a Small Company... 73
No One is 15% Smarter... 73
Developing All Your Skills 74
Assume Goodwill 74
Mental Mentors 75
Beware of Experts 76
Two Kinds of Jobs... 76
Be Truthful 77
Sometimes Your Passion... 77
How To Be Positive... 78
Get a Bad Job Before... 79
The 5% Rule 79
How To Find a Mentor... 80
Summer Doldrums... 81
The Anti-Graduation Speech 82
Five Resolutions You Can... 83
What To Do When... 83
Dear Kid, On Being... 84
10 Lessons a Dad... 85
Bad Career Advice... 86
A Fifth Grade Do-Over 88
Coaching Little League... 88
How To Be More Likeable... 89

Ch 5: If you want to start a company: 100 mini-lessons 97

Ch 6: Best and worst career advice from other Dads 117

About The Author 146

Foreword

You could burn an entire aisle of career books at a major bookstore and see nary a wisp of wisdom rise from the smoke. But you'd be doing us all a favor, because the world doesn't need all those books about jobs and job hunting. In fact, we all worry too much about interviews, resumes, job ads, and key words. We all worry too much about looking for jobs, finding jobs, and changing jobs.

We don't think enough about doing work and making profit. In today's economy, the only way you're going to keep a job or get a job is by showing how you will do your job in a way that makes your employer successful.

So what's this? Another career book? Nah. My good buddy G.L. Hoffman would never waste his time writing a career book. What he has produced is a slew of precious little lessons that will transform your life by changing how you look at work, think about work, do work and profit from work.

G.L.'s experience makes him the best coach you will ever meet. As a serial entrepreneur G.L. has created managers from scratch. He has built companies one job applicant at a time. G.L. has survived and thrived through downturns, upturns and sideways economies. He has advised the smartest company founders and trained the lowliest staffers who just got out of college. He knows how business ticks because he has spent his life winding up new little companies (and their employees!) and sending them out to prosper and make money.

How does he do this? Ah, to find that out you have to follow the funny orange dog and dig into this book. G.L. won't find you a job or fix your resume. But, one by one, he lays out the little lessons you need to get ahead, like building blocks. He shows you how success grows when you put one bit of wisdom on top of another every day while you work.

If you haven't figured it out yet, what I'm telling you is that G.L. is a mentor. He builds companies by building people. This book is his advice. These lessons are for people who want to work – not to have a job, but to produce profit for their employers and for themselves.

Don't burn all those career books we talked about… but stop worrying about job hunting and interviews and resumes. Dig every morsel of wisdom that G.L. has put into this tightly-packed book. I've known him for years, but it would take lots more meetings, lunches and quiet talks to learn as much from G.L. as you'll find in this book. Like that funny dog, I'm digging it again and again. Start digging!

– Nick Corcodilos, www.asktheheadhunter.com

Introduction

Most of us work. Many of us start working as teenagers and never stop until we retire or, heaven forbid, lose our jobs.

How we actually do this work is pretty much left to us. We learn from good and bad bosses, co-workers and customers, and other advice-givers. Some of it is good, some isn't.

The best learning, of course, comes with experience. Over years of working, each of us learns what works at work, and what doesn't. We apply those lessons starting about mid-career when we become the most productive and valuable to our companies and bosses.

Older workers and mentors are agreeable to sharing these lessons. Trouble is, those who need the lessons the most are the least receptive to them.

Whereas the content of the lessons are generally good and helpful, often the stodgy presentation skills of the messenger don't help.

In today's media rich environment any advice method must be clutter free and to the point. Which is why this book contains over one hundred short mini-essays which will give the reader just enough advice.

Every once in a while, most of us will have to look for a new job. Since we do it so infrequently, we really are not very good at it. Using the same concept, there are short paragraphs in the book for the job seeking reader. These are not intended to replace the work of skilled career coaches. But some of the ideas are easily implemented and are exactly what you need. These are basic 'learnings' that will help you hit the ground running in your job search effort.

Thanks to Brad Shorr of Word Sell, Inc., who brought me the idea of designating the most relevant tips for today's currently employed as Recession Protector Tips. We have identified these RPT's throughout the book with one of JobDig's mascot dogs.

There are numerous resources out there for the general job seeker. At JobDig, we are fortunate in having many of these resources as contributors to our weekly jobs newspapers, websites, and career centers. At the bottom of each page, we have listed the url of some resources that can help you in your search,....because everyone should dig their job.

Chapter 1:

On the job improvement tips

Ten New Year's Resolutions You Can Keep

1. **Get to work on time.** Nothing is simpler and nothing makes a statement more than being on time. The reason? Being consistently late to work, although no big deal in your mind, sends a negative message to your boss.

2. **Stay positive.** Within reason, don't be all giddy and stupid positive acting. Just remain positive about your business, your company, your co-workers and your specific job. Again, it is a simple thing to do. A minimum performance standard.

3. **Don't gossip.** Gossip is the hobglobbin of small minds. Don't go there.

4. **Learn something new every day and every week.** Advancement is all about improving your skills. No matter what your current job, you can learn a new skill. This one is up to you. Think small, incremental skill development…they all count and add up.

5. **Do something nice for a co-worker or customer…that is extra-ordinary.** And, here is the tough part: expect NOTHING in return. Don't even hint at some kind of quid pro quo.

6. **One day a week, dress one level up from your normal dress code.** In grade school, we used to call it 'wearing your Sunday school clothes' one day to school on dress-up day. I am sure that dates me. One guy here wears a tie (we are very casual here at JobDig) on Tuesday. He calls it Tuesday Tie Day. No one told him to do it—he just does it. We notice it.

7. **Do 10% more.** Simple and achievable.

8. **Tell your mom and dad about your workplace.** What you do. What your company does. What you are learning. Being a dad myself, (duh!), I love hearing about my kids' workplace. Dads —and Moms—appreciate this…and you may be surprised, they may even have some ideas for you to implement.

9. **Do something beneath your pay grade.** In the military, this is when the general stops the car and picks up some trash along the road. Too good to make coffee? How about cleaning the pot?

10. **Make it a point of being known for your manners.**

JOBDIG RECOMMENDS: www.jobsearch.about.com

Be a Job Improver Instead of a Job Seeker

Much has been written about being a job seeker. But there isn't much on being a job improver. In another words, if you are not satisfied with your current job, how can you improve it? Are there things you can do to make your job better. If you try these suggestions, you might not find yourself being a job SEEKER.

1. **Look for work.** Some upper managers I know describe employees with the shorthand version of this..."he sees work." What this means, is that this employee does not have to be told every little thing to do. He/she is engaged and can find something productive to do.

2. **Change your attitude.** A lot of times, one can improve the current job by simply changing your attitude. Be positive. Think positive. Show some energy! The world is full of boring, ho-hum people, you can make a new name for yourself by being a sunshine pump at work.

3. **Look for new ideas to help your current business.** I don't care if you have not been known up til now as an idea generator....it is never too late to start. Can you see something that should be done a different way? How about a new customer who you might know? Maybe you see a new product that your company can offer? It is just important to try? Not all your ideas have to be good ones...just try, throw them out there. No right minded business manager will ever say...'no, don't give us any ideas.' Business succeeds with new ideas. Learn to get new ideas, and even more importantly...how to present them.

4. **Read more.** Are you becoming an expert in your area, or about your company? Do you understand the market you serve? By reading more, and becoming more knowledgeable about your company, industry and marketplace, you will have better ideas, and will soon become known for it. I think this is a big mistake that a lot of younger people make...they assume that the managers know 'everything'...far from it...take the lead here and find your way to success.

5. **Ask your manager/boss.** Let them know that you are committed to the business. You want to improve, and do better and more. Notice I said do better, and then do more? Most of the time, there is plenty of room for you to improve your own job by simply doing better work, faster, more error free, and so forth.

Try this before jumping off the job cliff...

JOBDIG RECOMMENDS: www.asparker.com

What To Do When The Boss Ignores You

This happens too frequently. The issue is, basically, that you want either more direction or more recognition for your work and effort, right? There are several realities happening here. Contrary to most business books and management advice gurus, the workplace is full of managers who do not understand their job. Their job, succinctly stated and oversimplified, is to get work done through others. Nothing more.

How they achieve that is the difficult part. Most managers try…they read books, model their own bosses' behavior, even go to seminars and classes Trouble is, they often do a lousy job…and now, they have been promoted, typically because a) they have seniority or b) have done an 'ok' job and have moved up the ladder.

Now, you are bright and bushy-tailed (Who says THAT anymore?) and you actually came into the job wanting to be the best employee you could be for the company. Now, your boss ignores you, and you feel left out, under-appreciated, unfulfilled…and, even worse, you are wondering if you are stuck in a job with no future. Sounds grim. So, what are some steps you can take right now?

1. **First, get a grip.** "MAN UP." This is not grade school. This is the real world. No one is going to hold your hand. This is under your control.

2. **Make a list.** List on one side all the reasons you can think of why your boss might be ignoring you. Could one reason be that your work is above standards, and he feels you do not need any direction or help? Or, is he or she really simply a bad manager? Did you turn a project in with errors one time?

3. **On the other side of the list, list three ideas for solving each of the things on the left side of the page…these three ideas must be in YOUR control.** Think about every thing YOU can do to help your boss manage you better. What can you do to fix each reason?

4. **Once you understand that the underlying issues, the better you will be in figuring out how to deal with it.** After you make this list—on one side, are all the reasons why you think your boss is ignoring you, and on the other side, are your ideas on how to handle each one, you are ready for the final step.

5. **Last step.** Communicate your plan to your boss. Don't hesitate, get angry, be defensive or accusatory. Be reasoned and logical. Take charge. Own the problem.

This is the hardest thing for people to handle. Most of the problems we encounter in the workplace are ours, not someone else's. It is much easier to think that others are the cause of our pain and suffering. Unfortunately, this is not the case. Be someone who figures it out. You will be further ahead.

JOBDIG RECOMMENDS: www.puresoapbox.com

How to Be Excellent in Meetings

I hate meetings. I much prefer one on one meetings or at the most 3-5 people meetings. Much more than that, and the meetings tend to get unfocused and de-generate into informational type meetings, which is fine, but nothing much gets done…or acted upon.

If your company has regular meetings, here are a few ideas that may help you:

1. **Always take good notes.** And try to keep them organized.

2. **Volunteer to write up the meeting notes.** No one likes doing this anyway, and your volunteering will stand out. The person who writes the notes will become THE most important person who attended the meeting.

3. **Stay positive and build upon others' ideas.** If you are a rain cloud in the meeting or throw cold water at everything said…you will find yourself outside the door and not on the inside.

4. **Smile and act enthused and engaged.** I know this is simplistic but too often I look around at meetings and you would think we just announced a big lay off or something. Lighten up. Take some personal responsibility for the attitude in the meeting.

5. **You do not have to agree with everything the bosses say.** Some bosses may want 'yes people'—most don't.

6. **Don't keep checking your watch during the meeting.** This is rude and perceived that way.

7. **Do not even think about bringing your cell phone into the meeting.** And, especially, do not place it on the table.

8. **Do not bring food into the meeting.** A drink is fine, but no food.

9. **Come prepared.** With everyone being busy, more often than not, most people will just attend the meeting. I knew someone once, who would actually prepare for the meetings where he was not even going to be on the agenda. This preparation allowed him to basically take over when the discussion on a certain topic arose. This one thing advanced his career substantially. True story.

10. **Be a sunshine pump after the meeting.** Try to find something positive to comment upon after the meeting. Pick one person to compliment after the meeting. A simple "good point today" will be remembered. Pass along good feedback.

JOBDIG RECOMMENDS: www.greatmanagement.org

Wondering How to Do Your First Big Presentation?

Clues: $5. Get one.

Here is the first one: Do not under any circumstance think about a professional presentation. Do something unusual and fun that rocks the boat. Make people stop and notice you. This is not to say that you do something stupid...the core ideas have to be there, shessh. BUT make them remember you. Have some fun. Be creative.

Someone has to get excited about it and it might as well be you. Show me someone who can present well...and get a staff energized and I will show you a future star.

Keep Learning to Get Ahead

Do not make the mistake of thinking that now that you have the job, that the learning stops. Far from it, to have a long lasting, meaningful career, you need to keep advancing your knowledge about your field.

School teachers take classes and seminars to maintain currency, tradespeople learn the latest in specialized fields, even attorneys are required to take so many hours of continuing education to keep current. What are you doing to maintain your competitive edge?

If you cannot afford to take some available classes at the local college, check out community programs. Often, they will have a class on Microsoft Word or Excel, maybe even an illustrator type class. Even if it is NOT in your job description now, I guarantee that sometime knowing a new program will help you in a job. Plus it always helps you because you keep your mind fresh. It is always good to better understand other areas of the business–knowing an accounting program will help you understand the financial area, somewhat.

You have to exercise your brain. Keep forcing new things, new ideas, new concepts, new learnings in...and receive rewards that you have not considered out.

JOBDIG RECOMMENDS: www.draudreycanaff.com

Work is Not Just an 8-5 Thing

Your responsibility as an employee is to be ready for a full day's work. Too often, I see people who come in to work on Monday morning not really ready to work. Maybe they partied too long on the weekend, or flew home on the Redeye, I am not sure.

Your responsibility is to prepare yourself both physically and mentally for the workday. Think of it this way, would you go on an important job interview with bloodshot eyes and being over-tired from the weekend? Then why, after you get the job do you treat it with such disrespect?

Telling Time or Building Clocks

My friend 'Jag' is a seasoned executive who knows exactly what he is good at, and what he can offer a company.

He is creative, smart, insightful and fun too. Any company would be glad to have him, IMHO.

Trouble is, he is very selective—he won't just work anywhere. He has decided that he works best in an environment of "clock builders," not "time tellers," is how he says it. I learned this earlier in my career too, although I couldn't say it as well.

The trick it seems to me is to find work that allows you to make an impact on the business, on sales, on people, or whatever, on a continuing, evergreen basis. In other words, figure out how your contributions or work product/output pay off for your employer even when you are not working. So, when you leave at night or on vacation, the work that you have done is still contributing to the organization.

If you are stuck in a telling time job, chances are good that you are stuck there for your own reasons. Most jobs are bigger than the people who fill them. You can gain control and start building clocks. If you want to, that is.

Plus…most good clock builders started out being time tellers. It is awfully hard to build clocks if you can't tell the right time.

JOBDIG RECOMMENDS: www.careersolvers.com

How To Handle the Negative Performance Review

I am sure you can prepare yourself for your performance review. Most are done annually, although some are done more frequently. Your future might be determined not only by the review, but how you handle it.

Too often, I have seen people get defensive, and even begin to argue point by point. This might make you feel better at the moment, but I am not sure it leaves a lasting positive impression.

Some of this depends on the size and formality of your company. Bigger companies have a process in place, typically, with all kinds of mechanisms for what to do prior, during and after the review. Smaller companies typically do not. Small companies review you more frequently, less formally, and you can be almost blind sided by negative comments.

Today, we are in an atmosphere of feedback. We all want feedback…or we say we do. But what we really want is positive feedback. We want to be told we are doing a good job and are a positive contributor.

Some small business owners give positive oriented reviews…but, I dare say, some give realistic and even harsh feedback. These business owners do not have time to massage feelings so that yours are not hurt. They want you to get better.

I think the key is to understand that the boss will have your best interests in mind. But he or she will also understand more than you, the goals of the company and your role in it…and, more to the point, his expectations of you. You want to know and understand these changing expectations.

You should want all kinds of feedback. Only by understanding how your performance is impacting your organization can you hope to do better. So, the next time you hear a review that hurts you, realize that it is most likely done only to help you get better.

You can pout, even quit if your feelings are hurt. Or, you can get better.

JOBDIG RECOMMENDS: www.beckoncall-coach.com

Are You Anonymous at Work?

No one wants to be anonymous. We all want recognition and appreciation for who we are, and what we do. Most of the surveys say that recognition is what we most crave from our workplace. And, it is the determining factor to why people stay at their job.

How can you make sure you are not anonymous at work, how can you stand out amongst all the others? Here are some ideas for you to try:

1. **See work.** In most companies, jobs are almost always bigger than the person. You can make your job bigger and better by simply seeing work that needs to be done, and then do it. Most of us work in small companies…there is always work to do. Do not wait around for someone to point out work to you. Get a reputation as someone who can see work, especially un-assigned work.

2. **On time.** Be on time in everything you do. Complete projects when you say you will. Show up on time in the morning or after lunch. This is a small thing, making this a workplace habit will pay off.

3. **Be perfect.** Understand that even though no one is perfect, your boss expects perfection. You never know when your poor grammar in an email will negatively affect your career. Learn to be your own worst critic. Always improve.

4. **Can do.** Exhibit a "can do" attitude. Remember that the company can pay a lot of people a lower salary to NOT do your work.

5. **Do the job no one else wants.** Careers have been made on this reputation alone…do the toughest, the worst, or the jobs that have caused others to fail. Search out the tough tasks.

6. **Be sales minded.** Most companies need revenue. What can you do in your job to add sales? Always be looking for ways that you can impact sales in your company. I guarantee you there is no faster way to move ahead in a company that being seen as someone who can meaningfully impact the sales.

7. **Customer-focused.** How does your job impact the company's customers? If you don't know how, find out. Every business needs customers. And every job touches the customer in some manner. Become an expert on how your job positively impacts the customer.

8. **Always improve.** Improvements do not have to be gigantic to gain attention. Make sure that this month you are doing a specific task better than you did it last month. Small incremental improvements in your performance get noticed.

JOBDIG RECOMMENDS: www.bartongoldsmith.com

9. **Don't whine, gossip or complain.** Save whining for after work and only to your partner, spouse and only if you absolutely need to. It is so common for people to get together and complain about work. The more you do, the worse you will do.

10. **Become an evangelist.** Most businesses have a leader or boss who is really-really-really good at presenting the business in an exciting, positive way. You can also do it, even if only to your co-workers, customers, family, friends. Think of it this way. You meet someone at a family reunion and they ask you what you do. What do you tell them? Does this person leave the conversation understanding more about your job and company? The goal should be to get THEM as excited about what you are doing and your company as what you are. Young people make think this is NOT cool, I understand. But in small companies, especially, your boss knows who are evangelists for the company.

How To Handle Negative People at Work

Have you ever worked with someone who can find the most negative way of looking at any idea? It can be very frustrating, especially if the negative person is your boss...and you are trying your best to improve the business and your own role in it.

Here are some things you can do if you find yourself in that situation:

1. **Do not let them win by losing your own energy for presenting new ideas and concepts.** Remember that it always easier to criticize than create. Keep trying.

2. **Make them part of the process earlier.** Often times, you wait too long to communicate your ideas. Some people simply need more time to process the idea...bring them in on its development. You may have to be more collaborative in the process...but, hey, is it more about you or the idea anyway?

3. **Ignore the criticism...on the outside.** But listen to it and make the adjustments. Once you fix the concerns, you are closer to your goal. Most nay-sayers cannot keep up with an ever-changing and improving idea.

4. **I want to repeat myself: Do not allow the nay-sayers to win, to beat you down**...keep pushing and stay positive...and keep learning, watching. It may well be your presentation skills that need the work, not the idea.

JOBDIG RECOMMENDS: www.more-opportunities.blogspot.com

Get Engaged At Your Job

One of the best career moves you can make is completely under your control.

Too often, we worry about our career path (if you are wondering about this too much, you are not on it, BTW), instead of making the most of each job experience we have. It is enormously gratifying to watch our own workforce, made up mostly of people in their 20's, finally seemingly 'get it' and actually get engaged in the work here.

The best career move you can make is TO GET ENGAGED AT YOUR JOB. If you can do this, or learn to do this, you will OWN the world of work. In short, in the words of a young kid I know…U ROK!

Here are some tests to see if YOU are engaged at your work:

1. **Do you care enough about 'the work' to NOT care who gets credit?**

2. **Do you go out of your way to help others, with absolutely no thought of getting something in return?** You are doing it solely to help a co-worker and the company.

3. **When times get tough, or you are confronted with an issue or problem that you cannot solve, what is your reaction?** Do you give up?

4. **Do you do the work assigned to you but do with it with such goodwill, creativity and positive attitude that even the most mundane tasks get completed with flair?**

5. **Are you a clock watcher?**

6. **Do you have fun at work?** Enjoy being there?

7. **Do you make suggestions?** Are you always thinking of new ways to improve the business, even if it is not in your area?

8. **Do you talk about your work at home or to your friends?** Do your parents say "Boy! Johnny really likes it there at _____!" Are your friends envious?

9. **Do you attract more work?**

10. **Do you seek to set a new standard at your job?**

Make it a point to get more engaged at work. After all, you already spend eight hours a day there, why not make it the best eight hours you can?

JOBDIG RECOMMENDS: www.the4realities.com

The Art of Getting Ahead

Ever notice how some people always seem to get ahead while others seem to plod along, doing good, but not exceptional work? What is the difference? How can you make a name for yourself, even if you are 'average?'

Here is one absolute law of the workplace: After the work (project, task) is finished, someone ALWAYS has a better idea. Many people find this frustrating. "Why does he always have these ideas AFTER I am finished? Why doesn't he tell me before I have spent all this time and money getting it to this point!!!"

You can complain about this law, but wishing will not make it go away. Recognize this law early in your career and you can make any job better and more productive. There are no small jobs, so if you embrace this law and understand how you can make it work for you, the opportunities will open up for you.

Here is how. In any project or task you do, get out ahead of the project. Make the job bigger, do not settle for doing it as expected. Make sure you accomplish the basics, but add your own inputs to it. Pixar, Steve Jobs' animation movie studios, has even institutionalized this idea. They have a department called "plussing." This department only looks at projects that are all done and completed. Their job is to search and find "Plus Ideas." These added small details often create a winning movie versus an average one.

Real world example: Here at JobDig, we give our customers and prospects a cute little plush dog, that looks just like our logo. Our customers love the dog, request replacements, and offer up all kinds of suggestions on ways we can use him in our business. Most businesses might have a nice logo, ours happens to be a cartoon dog. He is in this book. So, our plus concept was to make him into a plush toy and give him away. The next plus idea was to send him out via the mail, but not in a standard box. That would have been too easy. We thought it's a dog, so why not send him out in a doghouse shipping carton? This plus idea demonstrated that we are engaged, that we 'get' the humor behind our dog.

Are you with me so far? After the doghouse had been designed and created, we took another look…even though we were proud of our work, we were still intent on adding one more thing to make this idea (let's send our customers a plush dog) an even better one. We needed one more Plus. What did we do? We punched air breathing holes in the dog house roof. Perfect! What had been a simple job of sending the dog out in a "normal" box was improved and plussed several times.

JOBDIG RECOMMENDS: www.yourvirtualresource.com

Did every customer 'get it?' Did every recipient see the air holes in the direct mail package? No. But one of our content providers (we have regular JobDig contributing writers), told me when he received the dog in the doghouse, he noticed the air holes RIGHT AWAY and thought to himself, 'these guys get it." If you want to 'get it' at your job, find your own air holes. Do the expected, but stretch yourself and do more.

Wrong Job or Just Bored?

Is that it, or are you just not seeing the bigger picture? What is the potential of your job if you looked at it in a different way? A lot of young people quit a job too early thinking that their broad range of experience has taught them to understand the workplace. Here are some quick ideas to see if your boredom is the result of your job or your own perspective:

* Have you honestly tried everything to insert some excitement and passion into the work you do? It is not enough to think that the company is passionless. That only tells me that it needs someone to create passion. It might as well be you.

* Are you bored because you need constant reinforcement or feedback on how you are doing? This is not Little League any more, a lot of managers are working too hard to hand-hold you through your early years of working. Recognize that you have to find your own worth, your own way of measuring yourself, of finding small achievements that you can be proud of daily.

* Is the job itself made up of mundane boring tasks, easily mastered and, therefore, boring? Every job is important to someone. If you have mastered it but are faced with many, many more months of repeating the same task, over and over again, you might not like how that sounds. Most companies have certain business processes at work, and absolutely require someone who can accomplish the assigned tasks in the assigned manner.

Your challenge is to make the work better, more efficient, less costly, more impactful, something that can break you out of the rut. Try to achieve more in your daily work than your manager or company believes possible. Often the path to a meaningful career begins when you show how well you can perform a task or series of tasks.

Once you have mastered something, seek greater responsibility and perform well at the next set of tasks. Remember that your job is important to your manager and your company. If it is not important to you, it might be to someone else.

JOBDIG RECOMMENDS: www.maketheirday.com

Do You Have a Clap and Cheer Job?

There are no small jobs. Each job can be exciting, fulfilling and rewarding. Many times it is how you view your job that counts.

Some people see their job in a completely different light than anyone else. We all have seen the receptionist who takes it upon herself to be the best possible receptionist, greeting everyone with enormous goodwill. Everyone in the company understands and appreciates her role and considers the job and HER an important factor in their success.

I am reminded of the old story about the mother who was picking up her seven-year-old from school. That day, the teacher was going to pick the kids who were to be in the class play and this mother was nervous that her son would not get picked. If he wasn't picked, what would happen to his self-confidence, she wondered. The little boy bounced out of the school, with a big grin on his face, and said "guess what, Mom? I have been picked to clap and cheer."

Even if you are not chosen to be in a lead role, you can always be a positive supporter. I imagine you will earn your spot in the future.

Small Companies are Better

For those of us in small companies, we cannot literally imagine working in a big one. Here is the ultimate irony:

People in small companies cannot imagine working for a big company, perhaps, but down deep they do have a bit of an inferiority complex, and are really wondering if they can handle the professionalism and systems of a larger company.

People in large companies think they can work in a small company just fine, thank-you-very-much. And not only work, but contribute almost immediately, and will soon DOMINATE the other lesser folks.

At last count, there were about 20 million small businesses in the USA, and most of us work in a small business. Master working in a small business and your chances are good you can find another one, somewhere, someplace, sometime.

JOBDIG RECOMMENDS: www.eduplan.us

They Yelled at Me for Reading a Magazine

I am sure there are some jobs that are so boring and mundane that one could read on the job and still not have their work suffer too much. No, wait a minute. Actually, I can't think of a single job where that is the case.

Just because you haven't been told what to do, that doesn't mean you have the option of doing whatever you want at work. Ask for more work from those around you, or go looking for extra work. I am sure the extra work is out there. Go clean something if that's all you can find. Chances are pretty good that if you ask for more work from enough people, you can find something extra to do and feel more productive and helpful. More than likely, you are being just lazy.

I Want To Quit After Only a Year, Is That OK?

Years ago that was true. If a candidate jumped around from job to job, it was certainly something to look at more closely. The thinking was that the candidate had some recurring issue or just was an unhappy sort of employee. This has changed over the past few years. Now, the entire work force is temporary in that jobs change so frequently that it is not unusual for a workforce to turn more frequently than historical averages.

What is more important is for you to have a heart to heart discussion with yourself to keep your current job and your attitude about it in perspective. Keep in mind your current company has probably made an investment in you and your training. You might be hitting your stride, becoming a more productive part of the workforce for your employer - it's almost unfair for you to leave after you have taken advantage of some training and development. What is apparently a good career move might actually be a step backward or down.

So it is not judged the same way as it used to be, but one cannot tell too much about a job even after one year. Give it some time, work a bit harder and smarter, see if something else at the employer might be more to your liking and, of course, you can always talk to your manager or supervisor about your feelings. You might be surprised at their advice.

JOBDIG RECOMMENDS: www.rethinkingwork.com

How To Cope With Criticism at Work

So you are being criticized by a manager or your boss and not a co-worker? Some of your problem might be historical conditioning. How have you been challenged in the past? Have you been able to adapt to different feedback styles? Think back to the coaches you have had. Were you able to learn better from one particular coach more than any other?

The point is, just like there are different coaching styles, there are different management styles. Generally speaking, and this is a real generalization here, the earlier you are in your career, the less likely it will be that you have a manager who is nice and cuddly. Expect to be challenged; that is part of growth and of pushing yourself to the next level. On Coach Bobby Knight's TV show, he said that the teachers he had in his life who made the most impact were the ones who were intolerant of mistakes. So if you have a boss who is criticizing you, why not make the assumption of goodwill and assume he or she is only trying to make you better at your job.

As far as coping with it, if you think more positively about it, you can handle it better. And do not make the mistake that a lot of younger people make, thinking that older bosses are less observant. They can most certainly pick up on your body language. If you are handling the conversation poorly, and feel unfairly persecuted or just cannot handle criticism well, your boss is getting that message too, loud and clear. Is that the message you want to communicate?

Plussing

We believe in a lot of sales training. We like to train our reps for about an hour each day. We have a real commitment to it and our plan depends upon each rep getting better at their job.

More than that, I think most of our reps understand the commitment we are making. Certainly it is in our own interest to improve their performance, but there is no question that their individual skills are ever-improving. I think we are giving them an MBA in sales, frankly.

I am struck by how some job candidates seem to be unaware that it is NOT just the job that they are getting. It is what you learn while doing it. Are you making yourself better? Improving a lifetime skill? Does the company seem committed

JOBDIG RECOMMENDS: www.workplace-excellence.com

to training you and not just product training? Find out and assign some significant value to it. Next time, drill down on these training-improvement issues and not just the obvious facts about the job.

Employers Must Earn Your Loyalty

Much has been written about employees working hard, performing for their company and earning their place at the table. Companies demanded improvements in efficiency and production.

These days, more employers are recognizing that this is not a one way street. Employers have to work hard FOR their employees too. Yesterday, I had lunch with a headhunter friend who reminded me that for Generation Y workers, they are less concerned about what career move is next. "They have too many options," he said. "And the confidence in their own abilities and marketability. They are in control."

So, if you are in that age group...how can you make YOUR employer earn your loyalty, commitment and hard work. Here is what we try to do at JobDig to constantly earn the rights to the efforts of our people, many of whom are in this Generation Why group.

First, we insist on an atmosphere of complete trust and respect. This is hard to pull off and manage, but it comes naturally if you hire the best quality managers. And people. Fakes are easy to spot. I think that is why one of our managers gets calls from parents of employees when they get into trouble. Trust comes from consistent and fair treatment.

Next, commit to training. We all want to improve and learn new skills. The twentysomethings want to feel like they are getting better. Companies earn employee loyalty by training and by showing them what they can do to improve a lifelong skill. Don't be small-minded. If you are 'overly' concerned about IM'ing and MySpace browsing, you and your company simply don't get it. Let it go.

Lastly, be consistent, fair. We have very high standards here and do our best to apply them across the board, equally and fairly. We measure a lot of activities, metrics in today's parlance. Just like in life, the highest performers do get some slack, but the standards are never relaxed for anyone. We tend to simply like the better performers more. We used to say that a person would quit over a principle being violated, more than almost anything else. Nothing is more true today.

JOBDIG RECOMMENDS: www.davidmaister.com

Recognize and Fix Small Irritants to Get Ahead

My belief is the small, niche businesses almost always serve their customers better than larger competitors. We are finding this to be true at Job-Dig, as our main competitors are either the near-monopolistic daily newspaper or the larger job boards.

If you are a twentysomething starting out in your career, here is one way you can get recognized no matter what size your company. Every company has customer irritants…these are small, mundane things that customers hate…but no one ever seems to fix them. At smaller companies, we are so intensely focused on the customer and this experience, that we tend to root out each little irritant… the goal being obvious: the easier it is do business with us, the better. No little 'nit' is too small to avoid our attention.

I remembered this on Saturday night as we returned from vacation to the main terminal at Minneapolis. Due to delays and connections, we arrived at nearly midnight after hours and hours of travel. The carrier was Northworst Airlines. As many of you know, NWA dominates air travel in and out of the Twin Cities and have had more than their share of financial difficulties. But the small irritants are alive and well at Northwest. This is a perfect example of a small irritant that can be simply fixed if someone simply cared.

So, again,…put yourself in the shoes of the passengers on this flight…the flight was completely full, cramped seats, no food, etc…but that is not the 'nit.'

When we arrived at the terminal, we parked at the furthermost gate…I am talking almost to Iowa, the gate was so far. During the near mile walk to baggage claim, each time we passed an empty gate, walking passengers could be heard saying…"what was wrong with THAT gate?" Gate after gate after gate we passed… and we were the only plane arriving at this late hour. Grrrrrrrrrrr.

Then to make matters worse, once we got to the main terminal the closest stairway and escalator down to baggage claim was closed off. So we had to continue walking to the far end of the main terminal before we were allowed to go downstairs to the baggage claim area. Well, you say, I am sure the baggage claim was right at the bottom of those escalators…noooooooo. The baggage claim they used was waaaaaaaaaaay back under the first escalator.

I felt like I was on an episode of "Punked." About 200 passengers are totally pissed off now at Northwest Airlines. Not me…luckily I was able to "let it go."

JOBDIG RECOMMENDS: www.surpassyourdreams.com

Somewhere in the bowels of Northwest Airlines there is some young person who could make a name for themselves quite easily.

How Gen Y Can Handle the Baby Boomers at Work

First, assume that all baby boomers have A-D-D and are un-medicated.

1. While waiting for us to complete a required piece of your project, if it is due at some point in the future, gently remind us a few days ahead of time.
2. If you see us away from work and we are with our spouses, introduce yourself to our spouse first so we don't embarrass ourselves by forgetting your name.
3. If you wonder if we saw an important piece of competitive information posted on a competitor's blog or on MySpace, we didn't. Send it to us. You can use email, however, we are NOT stupid.
4. In meetings, make your important points early in the presentation and keep the number of important points to 3.
5. Act like you have never heard our business stories before.
6. Best suck up line ever: "You should write a book about all you know about our business."
7. Ask advice even when you already know the answer.
8. Try not to be condescending about some computer program thing-y, as in "you use the grouping function in Outlook, don't you?"
9. Don't forget that we know how to do three things on the computer: we can send and receive emails (we just discovered the 'find' feature; we can open up Word, but we can't use the correction feature) and we can Google things.
10. Don't try to explain gigabites.

That's about all for now. How 'bout them Bears?

JOBDIG RECOMMENDS: www.alphaadvantage.com

Little Overlooked Things Can Destroy a Company Culture

A company culture trumps its products, services, or even people. It is that important.I was reminded of this over the weekend when I was talking with someone who recently joined a local company. This company even has an external positive buzz about it. But it still has a negative culture.

He told to me that during his initial training, he noticed that there were printed lists on employees' cubes. These were things that employees should watch for. Typed memos that said things like....Number 3. Your boss will take your good idea and take complete credit for it. This was on several cube walls, and in public sight.

I am all for employee empowerment, letting people reach their potential and not micro-managing them. But I draw the line at this sort of disrespectful-in-your-face-us-versus-them attitude.

If you are a worker, or even a manager, and see this sort of thing happening at your company, what would you do? You can fix it...no matter your level. Here is how:

1. **Don't participate.**

2. **Ask if the person realizes how negative these things are to others.** That some of you are trying to do the right thing here, and this sort of thing has negative influence. It hurts you, embarrasses you. And, that it makes you less proud of where you work.

3. **If he or she doesn't take them down after being somewhat embarrassed, ask what you can do to help solve some of these issues that are being raised.**

If it is your company, or your department, do not tolerate this sort of festering to go on.

JOBDIG RECOMMENDS: www.loyaltyleader.com

Five Things To Do At Work Before Asking for a Raise

1. **Over-perform.** If you are simply doing the job you were hired for, that might not be enough. These days you not only have to do that job, but do it exceptionally well. I mean, not just exceptionally well...more like, no one has ever done this job like this before-well.

2. **Timing is everything.** It always seems to happen that someone will ask for a raise at exactly the wrong moment. There is a poor sales month or quarter... bad time. The boss is under the gun for a big new project from his boss – bad time. It's like the high school girl who gets grounded and then the very next day asks to go to her first overnight party – bad timing.

3. **Do not ask your co-workers what you should do or ask for.** It is so tempting to ask co-workers for their opinions...and what they believe you should do.

4. **Ask for more work before you ask for more money.** This is a sensitive topic because a lot of bosses will take this as a sign that they are not managing you well. But you need to show that you can handle more, and continue to handle the current workload. I know there are tons of projects around that someone can and should do. Be the one that gets those extra projects.

5. **Do the work no one else wants to do.** Every job or company has crummy stuff to do. Some people avoid it and it gets noticed. Do you take your turn making coffee? (yes it is these small things) Do you clean up someone else's mess – and not make a big deal out of it? Do you volunteer to drop something off at a client's business...and not ask what the mileage reimbursement program is? All little things that get noticed and recognized.

JOBDIG RECOMMENDS: www.drogrady.com

Who is Your Real Boss

We all have bosses.

Most of us have bosses who are formally 'in charge of us.' In addition, we have someone who influences, maybe even controls, our work life but, since they are NOT our direct boss, we think we can avoid managing up.

So what happens when you are working for your boss's boss on a project? Quite obviously, this 'boss' is someone you need to please and satisfy. You need to do a great job but how you do it will maintain trust and respect of your boss. Here's how:

1. **Keep your boss informed every step of the way.** Never assume that (your boss and his boss) two are talking and coordinating your work output. In fact, assume they are not talking.

2. **Never, ever assume extra attention means you are being groomed to replace your boss.** This is so tempting to think…after all, you are thinking that "finally, someone recognizes my natural abilities around here." Leave your ego at home.

3. **Do not dis your boss.** I realize you don't like him, and his boss may not too thrilled with him either. But don't go there. The more supportive you are of him, the better. Way better.

4. **Ask your boss for his help.** This is more than point number 1. Do not find yourself being isolated, no matter how important the 'project.'

5. **Don't brag about this new relationship to others.** This will spell disaster.

6. **Lastly, don't read too much into a simple request.** In more informal organizations, some bosses just like to make simple requests of people and they don't particularly care about the 'chain of command." It might mean that you were simply the one who answered the phone or nodded your head at the right time.

The boss of your boss is the easiest one to handle. The real mouse in the room is when you don't recognize another person's importance and choose to ignore a request. A CEO request comes to mind, that's easy. But a request for someone who is working with a customer? Ignore this person at your peril.

JOBDIG RECOMMENDS: www.donnacutting.com

Five Must-Do Things You Should Do Now To Avoid Being Laid Off

Pick up any fear mongering newspaper today and you will read about companies laying off hundreds, even thousands of workers. It can be a frightening period especially for those of us who feel like our continued employment is contingent upon market forces and not individual performance. Instead of worrying and waiting, what can you do now?

1. **Multi-task, multi-skill, multi-talent.** Sometimes it doesn't matter if you are the best left handed XRay technician in the clinic, if XRay technicians are being laid off, you are on the list. Remember that old joke about the two guys on safari being chased by lion..."think we can really outrun him?" one says to the other. "I don't care about HIM, all I have to do is outrun YOU," says the other. Same for people going through a layoff, all you need to do is be just a little more valuable than the other guy.

2. **Do a great job.** In most cases, the layoffs happen first to the average or mediocre performers. Get yourself out of that group NOW. You can sit around and worry, maybe even bitch and complain...but that won't pay for groceries or cable. Now is the time to work longer and harder.

3. **Get yourself ready.** This might mean save more of your current paycheck. It might mean to update your resume or take night courses. It might mean to start doing research on companies which are hiring in your space. When and if you get laid off, you want to be ready to go on your new job hunt. A favorite place to start is JobDig at www.jobdig.com where we list current job openings that are available. Another site is LinkUp.com. This is a site that aggregates jobs from company websites...NOT job boards. Both are worth a look.

4. **Remember layoffs are most definitely NOT personal.** Most layoffs are institutional and not personal and you should not take it that way. Most of the time, the reasons for layoffs are completely out of your control and jurisdiction. Obviously, you will go through a period of grief-like attitudes. Knowing that it is NOT you might help you. Start thinking this way now.

5. **Get busy.** Everyone can work harder at work. This is a fact. You should give yourself a bit of a pep talk. If you ever played sports at any level – this is the workplace equivalent of the halftime or pregame speech. I never had a single coach who played the "pity us, ain't it awful" game. Give yourself one of those brutally honest talks today and bust your ass. You might not avoid an upcoming layoff, but you won't be playing what-if, or woulda-shoulda-coulda with yourself later.

Good luck.

JOBDIG RECOMMENDS: www.epicliving.com

Should I Settle At My Job That I Think Might Be Making Me Miserable?

If there ever was a unifying question in today's workforce, it is this one. Here is my take on it.

First, everyone is different. If you have six months' of cash saved up, you have more options available to you than someone who is living paycheck to paycheck, with ramen being the sole nutrient for the day or two before payday. I get that.

We all live nowadays in a time of instant gratification. Some say the current crisis is caused by the housing problems, but we really all know that we each had a small part to play because we didn't want to save up for the newest iPOD (now in red!!), so we will just 'charge it.' The art of delayed gratification is understood, but seldom practiced.

Same with our jobs. We want instantly to be promoted and to be 'fulfilled.' We all want to be passionate about what we do. We want meaning. And we want it today. Dad waited for his 'fulfillment' after all, and look what happened to HIM.

But. Maybe your mom and dad didn't tell you this because we were too concerned with your own self worth development. You are used to performing and excelling, even if you didn't truly perform or excel.

Our bad. So now here we are. You are miserable at work, and you don't want to "settle." What to do? What to do?

I think you have to have a heart to heart talk with yourself, first. Are you giving it a chance? Have you worked hard enough at it? Do others at your job seem ok with it? Could it be YOU?

Most of the time, we can do better in our current jobs and try to jump out before we have finished learning as much as we can. So unless you have another, obviously better job waiting for you, here is something to realize and work on.

Every job is BIGGER than the person holding it. If you are creative, smart and realistic enough every job can be made BY YOU to be that non-misery creating job you so want. You have heard stories about even the lowest office assistant creating a new role for herself by doing extra things with an incredible positive attitude to the point where she becomes one of the most crucial members of the team….and she started in a near demeaning role. Even you can be in charge.

JOBDIG RECOMMENDS: www.jobdig.com

What's the Trick or Secret About Management

Chances are, you are about to join or have joined a company where the stated strategy is basically, somehow, with meetings (typically), strategy sessions (usually) and goals-missions-targets (daily) to get you and the other members of your team to perform better and in alignment with what the company needs to get done.

Some people do better in this environment than others. They are perfectly willing to belong to a group, especially one that can achieve more than they could have achieved alone. Sport teams are like this, each team member has his or her role, and they know that if everyone does their job, all win. Think about the baseball team–one missing fielder can spell trouble if that is where the other team hits the ball.

Companies are like that, traditionally. The trick in management has always been to somehow meld individuals into a fine, functioning team. Some management(s) are better at this than others, of course. The successful ones use a variety of methods and techniques, motivation and training to get this team to perform better.

Here is the interesting part, at least to me. Too many team members look to management, ie. the team leader/coach/boss, to make the team work. These team members say, in effect: It is 'their' job to train me, motivate me, teach me, explain things to me, manage me if 'they' want me to do THIS for 'them.'

Luckily, at my current company, most of the team members are taking personal responsibility for their skills development. They understand that skill development is the ticket to a successful worklife. Instead of sitting around and waiting for someone to give them the magic secret to success, they are working on it every day. I hope they know they are actually in charge of this.

JOBDIG RECOMMENDS: www.co2partners.com

What Bosses Like

Instead of being so me-oriented at work or in your career, have you stopped to consider what your boss likes or appreciates? The sooner you can determine that, the faster ahead you will get.

Some of you are saying, "Oh no, this is going to be a lesson in playing politics at work." Far from it, I have a sure-fire thing you can today that will serve you well in your career.

Some people have asked me about being an evangelist, which I wrote about in the first chapter (Are You Anonymous at Work). One person had a particularly insightful question… "How can I become an evangelist if I don't really feel comfortable doing it, or if I don't know the Company's long term goals? In order to be an evangelist, don't you have to a bit higher up and have a better understanding of all that a company does?"

Great question. First, all it takes to be an evangelist about your job or company, is to find a specific component that you are excited about. It might be your particular job, or service to a specific customer, or a company goal.

Once you can find this excitement point, practice talking about it. Make it short, simple, direct…but make it compelling. Think of this way: You meet someone at a family reunion, and they ask you what you do. Now, you probably say, "I work at ABC Company and I am in quality control." To become an evangelist, just add one sentence. "Let me tell you why I am excited about ABC and my job." Then talk in very human terms about your excitement point. "I am excited because they believe in daily training and I can feel myself improving every day." This technique is one step up from positive self talk, but it always works. Frankly, it is hard to say the phrase "why-I-am-excited" in a dull monotone. It forces you to act excited.

This was demonstrated to me early in my career at a Trade Show. We were exhibiting at a Show, and one of my sales guys had more leads, and more activity than all the rest of us. I had to find out what he was doing differently to attract all the interest. He had a clear, evangelist-type first question he was asking booth visitors. He would simply say, "Can I explain why we have the most exciting product at the Show today?" More than the words, was the attitude. He was excited to be there, and it showed. People like to be around positive, excited people.

Bosses like employees to be evangelists. Learn to be a sincere evangelist for your job and company…and notice how many people start to notice you.

JOBDIG RECOMMENDS: www.workmatters.com

Making Your Bones

Oldtime gangsters used the phrase "making your bones" to mean that in order to earn your way into the Mafia, you had to do something nasty.

Today, for interns in summer jobs, you are making your own bones by working at far less pay than normal and in exceptionally trying circumstances. Often, companies bend over backwards to create a job for you, the intern…most of us know what it is like to find a career area that you are passionate about, but lack the experience to find a job.

"Come back after you have had some experience," they say. We say, "how do I get that experience?" It is called internships.

Like the gangsters, these jobs can be quite nasty. You are expected to work like a full time employee, often for NO pay, or if you are being paid, for a minimum wage. Is the experience really worth it? It all depends.

If you can see a clear way to leverage the internship into a full time job, in an area that is difficult to break into, sure. I have a friend, actually a friend of my daughter's who wanted to work in television, actually in television NEWS. She was a recent college graduate, didn't even study TV and Radio in college…but still…she had what used to be called "gumption." Through a friend of a friend, she wrangled an UNPAID internship at a major network. She worked hard, never complained, did great work and after a year became an assistant producer to a nationally known news anchor…she books, interviews the people he interviews on-air. She is 25. I'd say that internship paid off.

I think the key in internships is to pick them right. Make sure you are working for someone who you will learn from and who has enough industry contacts to help you get that future job. If you can't afford to work for free, explain that fact, and let them know that you will be willing to trade some compensation for the experience…but that you still need to live and eat. Most people will give you something.

Then, once you are in the job, work hard…have I said that before?…it is that important. And, do the jobs that no one else wants to do. This is the fastest way to earn your bones.

JOBDIG RECOMMENDS: www.leadershipkeynote.net/consulting/high-org.htm

Advice You Won't Hear at Commencement

At graduation time and scores of commencement speakers will be giving out advice – some good, some not so good. If your frame of reference for the workplace is "*The Office*" – here are some other realities for you to consider.

First, attitude counts for far more than you have been led to believe. I know HR people who say "Hire For Attitude, Train the Skill."

Next, you are bringing a fresh perspective and a youngish attitude to your first job. There will be people who love it...and those who do not. Don't fret about it. Don't think everyone is out to get you. Don't change your personality or your willingness to take chances. But, and this is important: Understand that we have seen fresh ideas before – yours is not the first. And you may well be wrong.

Stay out of office politics. Every office has some internal policies, but avoid being known as a gossip.

Find a mentor. This does not mean you need to suck up to someone who is above you. But be on the lookout for someone who can help you, who can teach you.

Over-deliver. This is the one thing that will make or break you, IMHO. What does this mean? Simple: do the job better than 'they' are expecting.

And lastly – remember that every job is bigger than you believe. It is up to you to set a new standard for your own job.

Last minute tip to gain extra recognition: Be a clean freak at your workplace. I just saw our company microwave and nearly lost it. Your co-workers are not your mother. Clean up your own mess.

JOBDIG RECOMMENDS: www.resumelines.com

Good Luck With Being a Lone Ranger

Even the Lone Ranger had Tonto.

Other than close friends and family, do you have someone who is willing to give you advice, help and a kick in the ass when you need it?

Call this a mentor or a coach – it might be someone in your industry, a business friend, someone from church, a neighbor, whoever it is – they can offer you valuable insights on issues that we all face from time to time. If you let them – and if you take the first step.

For the longest time, I couldn't ask for this kind of 'connection' either. It seemed unprofessional and insecure somehow. Boy, was I wrong about that.

If you are hesitant and don't know how to take the first step, here's what I did. Maybe it will work for you.

1. **Watch and listen for someone who brings new insights and knowledge** – you want someone with different perspectives and backgrounds.
2. **Have they had some success?** Do you respect them? If they said "jump," would you say "how high?" or would you want to evaluate it even more?
3. **Ask for their advice.** It is literally this easy.

There is one thing people cannot seem to resist – and it is giving advice and/or help. May I ask you for some advice? – always works.

Making Chicken Salad Out of Chicken$!#*

Attitude has a lot to do with success in the workplace. It trumps skill in most jobs.

But another talent, almost unrecognized but always appreciated, is an ability to take any negative thing and make it into a positive. Surely you know someone like this. It is not just that they are positive thinkers, it is more than that. This person is literally almost never stumped, never says "I give up" and always has found 'nother way 'round the barn. Every problem has a solution, they say.

So, how do you get to be a chicken salad maker? Five tips:

1. **Be creative**. What other problem is similar to this one? How was that one solved? Brainstorm.

2. **Don't wallow around in the problem area too long.** Some people keep stirring the problem bucket until it really starts to stink. Recognize and define the problem but don't add to it. Work on a fix, fast.

3. **If one solution is good, three is better.** Think multiple solutions and choose the best option. Think you have THE right solution?, take a deep breath and 'plus' it with one more element or thought.

4. **Don't be hesitant about sharing your chicken salad idea.** Even in its rough form, try it out on someone. Don't think it has to be perfect quite yet.

5. **Do it enough and you'll get more and more chances to develop this skill.**

You won't see this on any resumes, but I want chicken salad makers in every level of my company.

JOBDIG RECOMMENDS: www.partnerinperformance.com

Chapter 2:

Preparing for a new job

Interview For the Job You Don't Want

One of the best pieces of advice in Dick Bolles' *What Color is Your Parachute?* is to interview for the job you actually do not want.

Why? Practice.

Why wait for the perfect job opening? Apply at a few jobs that you even might be over-qualified for…and definitely those jobs that you cannot see ever fitting you. The concept is that you will learn how to respond to questions and how the interviewer reacts to each. This practice interview can do wonders to get you prepared for the prime interview…which you must ace.

How To Find Your True Passion at Work

Easily said, hard to achieve. Most of us have no clue how to find our passion. We simply lack the ability to TIVO ourselves ahead a few years to see if THIS job could provide the passion.

So—how can you find YOUR passion, if you really don't know?

It is easy. First, what do you HATE doing? What kinds of jobs have you had that you hate?

In my own case, I was in the Air Force. One of my early jobs was as a missle officer. I literally managed a nuclear facility. The responsibility, as you can appreciate, was awesome, even intimidating. But there was one thing I HATED.

As you can probably understand, everything we did at the missle complex was 'by the book.' There were no options, none, for creativity at the missle silo. You can appreciate that, right? I hated it….and decided then and there, I would not work somewhere that was so regimented, so by the book.

So what do YOU HATE? Make a list…then make a list of exactly the opposite. Chances are, you will get closer to finding your true passion.

JOBDIG RECOMMENDS: www.jobmarketsecrets.com

You Don't Get In the Locker Room by Buying a Ticket

A lot of first time job seekers believe that once they have spent all that time on their cover letter (Dad, what do you think about this, how about this?, this?, this?) and then their resume (Does this font look better, should I mention that one seminar I went to?), their job is over.

Companies, they feel, should be able to see by the sheer appearance and apparent giftedness of the writer, that they would make a great employee.

Earth to job seekers: This is not the case. It is like you bought a ticket to the big game on Saturday. You get a seat and you get to watch. That's about it. If you think Charlie Weiss is going to scan the crowd, find you and then invite you into the Notre Dame locker room after the game for the postgame celebration...well, it is probably not going to happen.

Sending out a great cover letter and a great resume is about the same thing. It gets you in the game.

Ask Others About Their Careers

If you are unsettled about what you should be doing for a career, maybe you should take an interest in some other professions. Talk to people, find out how they like the job, the good and the bad.

It is fairly simple...just walk up to them and say, "I am thinking about becoming a nurse. Do you have time to talk with me about it?" Obviously, this works better if you actually are thinking about becoming a nurse.

Most people are more than happy to talk about their jobs, how they decided on this specific career, and will give you advice on the best path you should take to get there.

JOBDIG RECOMMENDS: www.cpcoaching.com

Five Things To Look For in Your First Company

Here at JobDig, we love to hire recent college graduates. We believe that our company culture fits exactly what a new graduate is looking for in a first job. Here is why:

1. **We train on a daily basis and use the latest training techniques.** More than that, our sales leader and trainer has been doing it for 30+ years! He knows his stuff. Make sure the leaders at your new company can teach you.

2. **We are fair, sincere and transparent.** Here's a great question to ask of any employer. Do you consider your practices to be fair to all employees?—See how they answer THAT one. Luckily, we are still a small company, under 100 people. We think it is important to make big decisions in front of all workers…we are not ashamed of anything we do. If we felt we had to hide things from our company and workers, something bigger is wrong.

3. **Everyone understands the business model.** Some first jobs are not like that. Can you tell your mom and dad how the business makes money in a specific, clear way? Business is all about serving customers…make sure you can articulate how your prospective business does it. If you can't say it easily, it more than likely is NOT you…but them.

4. **We are young, fast, quick and we make mistakes.** Hopefully, we learn from them. We do not shoot either messengers or people who make mistakes.

5. **We respect each other and it shows, even to the candidates who walk through our office.** We are playful, but respectful. And safe.

But that's just me.

Urgency in Your Job Seeking

You should always approach the job search just like it was your full time job. This means getting up at a normal, early time…and get started on the job search day.

My advice is to show some urgency. I believe urgency shows interest, passion, and an understanding that the opening is open but only for a short time. Some-

JOBDIG RECOMMENDS: www.jibberjobber.com

one will fill that job—you need to work hard to prove to the company that it had better be you.

As a hirer, I love to see applicants who WANT the job. In fact, we always tell candidates to "think about what we discussed, then call us back at a certain time." It amazes me to learn that a few people do not even hear that simple direction, and wait around hoping we will call them.

In short, it is ok to want the job and to communicate that to the person doing the hiring. Do not worry that they will think that you are some stalker-type person...far better to show interest and excitement in the potential job.

College Grads and Taking the Summer Off

Like Spring Break trips, cell phones for kids and $4 lattes, taking the summer off after graduating from college seems normal. It must have something to do with all the pain and suffering one has to fight through nowadays on college campuses. Now that the summer is about over, young 22-year and 23-year olds are starting to search for that all-important first job. Here are some quick tips:

1. **Sending out resumes to openings you see on the mega job boards will get you zero interviews.** That sounds like a generalization but it won't work.

2. **Ask your parents, their friends, your friends' parents and their friends for references and ideas.** It seems to me that the fastest way in the door is with a reference, preferably from a friend. It almost always works.

3. **If you do get an interview, show up.** SHOW UP. Too many times, we see people who just reek of I-don't-really-want-a-job attitude. It is so easy to be the one person who wants to work.

4. **Job hunting is a lot like work.** You can't do it later. Approach it like it is YOUR job and you will be miles ahead.

5. **Interview for the jobs YOU DO NOT WANT.** This is absolutely a must-do thing. What it gives you is practice for the real interview for the real job you want. Think of it as practice.

JOBDIG RECOMMENDS: www.jobgoround.com

Five Things To Do Now To Get the Best Summer Job

Spring break is coming up and soon students all over will be looking for that perfect job. Or, not. Most simply find a job close by, or that one that pays enough, or is easy to get. On the other hand, you want a summer job that is fun, exciting and interesting, here are five things you can do today that will help.

1. **Don't worry about your resume so much.** Today, resumes are basically devalued. And, your resume will not get you the job of your dreams. It is harder than that.

2. **Make a list that starts with this: "If I could, I would love to do {fill in the blank} this summer."** Make this fill-in-the-blank exercise fun, yet thoughtful. Stretch yourself...and make the list at least 20 items long. One young woman I know made her list... she wrote that she wanted to work on a TV show in New York City. She had NO experience, training, schooling, nothing...just thought about it. She landed herself an internship at a big network news show in NYC, and now, three years later, books guests for one of the nation's top political commentators. Here is a foolproof way to tell if you are thinking big enough. Share this list with your parents and friends. If they smile, or even laugh at your list, this is a good sign. Big goals do that.

3. **Now work hard at finding how to find your big, laugh-out-loud job.** Remember how you worked hard on that school project...this will take just as much time and effort. I was amazed at how my own kids would kill themselves over some school project, yet only want to spend about an hour finding a summer job.

4. **Don't forget to ask your parents and their friends for help, first.** We want to help you find this cool job. A job flipping burgers?, not so much.

5. **Be persistent, creative, unique, friendly, positive and-and-and-and, wait for it: Act like you deserve the summer job of your dreams.** Why shouldn't you get this job? Someone will, it may as well be you.

JOBDIG RECOMMENDS: www.workwrite.biz

I Just Graduated and I Don't Know What I Want to Do

Who cares? Just get started. Pick an area you think you might enjoy and just start chasing that down. Talk to people who work in areas you think you might like. Read books. Get on the web. Do anything and everything you can to start identifying jobs, careers, and places you might like to work. Chances are you will find something. Only about 2% of all adults that don't have work can't find a job, and I am thinking they don't want to find one anyway. Why do you think your entire life has to be planned out so meticulously? Like Steve Jobs says at Apple "life is a journey." Just do the best you can, learn as much as you can along the way, and don't repeat mistakes. But make plenty of them, mistakes like expecting someone else to figure out what you want to do. I wanted to play baseball for the Yankees. Well, that didn't work out so well for me either. Just jump in and start swimming.

Resume Liars

Resumes are de-valued these days, what with the ability to send out a million of them for $49. And, we all know that candidates tend to make even the lowest job seem glamorous on their resume. These are white lies and we can overlook them.

But what happens when someone outright lies? I actually caught someone in an outright lie, he had not even gone to the college he said he graduated from. Turns out, I had a college buddy who taught there, and I knew some of the local scene. When he couldn't comfortably talk about the area, I knew something was up. I even gave him some chances to say he had over-stated his resume. He didn't.

On the way out, I said... "you know, I think you could probably do the job. But – you know – I know you are lying about your college."

"So," he said, "if I admit it, will you still consider me?"

"No," I said, "it is one of the few unrecoverable mistakes you can make. Sorry."

That was in 1980. And I still believe I made the right decision.

JOBDIG RECOMMENDS: www.joanlloyd.com

Specificity Sells Even in Cover Letters

Sometimes in all the advice for jobseekers, we miss one important ingredient for your cover letter. In my mind, there is one thing that trumps all else:

Do not use a 'standard' cover letter. Find out something about the company to which you are applying, and make your cover letter stand out by referencing THIS company, an issue or, even better, a specific quality or thing you can bring to THIS job and to THIS company.

Here is an example: "I was reading about your chairman's message on your website and was interested in the new division that was created last year. In my resume, you will see that I have some experience in helping with the inter-company communications issues raised when a company creates a new division."

Specificity sells.

Job Seekers Should Know the Market

If you built bridges and ball fields, your job prospects in Minneapolis were fairly good. Word is, over 10,000 jobs were created in building the new bridge and in the two new stadiums here in the last year.

If, on the other hand, you are a newspaper reporter, chances are slim that the local daily papers are hiring. They are cutting and slashing with astonishing regularity.

Those are easy. Most jobs are not so clearly defined...customer service, warehouse help. Most are determined, not so much by the overall economy, but by the company itself. Tell me that an industry is down, i.e. not hiring and you can always find a company doing well. One that made some differentiating idea work in its business planning.

Your "job" as the jobseeker is to recognize those companies because they are always hiring, even when companies in their industries aren't. These unique companies use tough times to upgrade internal talent and skill levels. So, if you truly have a marketable skill, and can present it, the jobs are out there for you.

JOBDIG RECOMMENDS: www.swensonturner.com

Use a Strong Headline in Your Resume

HR people report they spend about 15 seconds on each resume. 15 seconds!

How can you ever hope to make your resume so appealing, so noteworthy that it makes it over to the next pile? The answer is NOT to print it on a toilet paper roll or some other dumb idea.

Instead of putting your name and objective at the top of your resume, try this technique: Make a single sentence headline about yourself that is so intriguing, funny, descriptive, unique, or creative that it breaks through the clutter and gets read. The hiring manager's reaction you want is, "I have to figure out more about THIS person." Typographically, make it bigger or bolder than anything else on your resume, so that it is the first thing read…remember you have 15 seconds.

So, how do you come up with the one sentence headline? Before you do that, do these four things:

1. **Leave your humility at home.**
2. **Read some magazine headlines and see what gets your attention.**
3. **If your mom or dad were asked to list three positive things about you, what would they be?**
4. **What are you most proud of?**

The perfect sentence would combine a specific reference to the job you are applying for, a skill you have demonstrated before and how you would apply that skill for them. Or, more simply, just make every word count. This is hard to do, so I have given you eleven examples:

1. **I married the prettiest girl in my small town high school,** proof positive I can sell myself; just think what I can do for the widgets of ABC.
2. **Voted 'most likely to succeed,'** when I should have been voted 'most likely to help ABC develop killer products.'
3. **I'm the eldest of five,** so I've always been the go-to person for extra work; hopefully, no one is still in diapers at ABC, and if they are, chances are I will be the first volunteer for this and other work that no one else wants to do.
4. **If I maintained my grades and juggled three jobs to pay my own way through college**, just think what I can do for ABC when I can really really concentrate on the customer service job.

JOBDIG RECOMMENDS: www.mediate.com

5. **I know who both Britney Spears and Carl Icahn are**, but if I don't know something, I can get the answer faster than you can say GOOGLE and ABC. So, you won't have to tell me how to do every little step along the way.

6. **I am not the kind who takes credit for things I don't do**—ABC has the perfect team spirit for me.

7. **I will never ask for a raise,** but I bet I will earn them at ABC, working hard.

8. **You can't know how good I will be for ABC,** yet; but I am confident there is no other candidate who knows more about PHP programming than me.

9. **I was MVP** for a state championship team in high school, voted on by my peers.

10. **I can tell someone's mood by the tone of their voice;** maybe you could use someone with my empathy skills in the customer service department of ABC.

11. **I am the kind of person who looks in snopes.com when I am sent forwarded 'factual' emails**, and I know which sender I can correct and who I shouldn't.

Brutal But Honest Post-Spring Break Advice

Ok, enough fun. Four (or five) years of skipping class, drinking too many tequila shooters, and re-working your myspace-facebook color scheme is about to come to a screeching halt. Some of you are worried that your 'education' won't actually pay off for you with the big bucks promised by that marketing professor. You know, the one who has never actually worked for a company. Well, sorry to say, his advice is the business equivalent of reading about Steve Jobs and thinking you are about to invent the I-Phone, dude. Sure, it could happen. But, in the meantime.... Here is some advice your parentals want to give you, but won't.

1. **Get serious about finding a job.** The last thing you need is to take a three month vacation after school. I know, I know. YOU worked hard and need to experience life a bit. Spare me. Mommy and Daddy just spent their retirement on your educational experiment so out of respect, the least you can do is go through the motions of becoming a real live, functioning, supporting yourself semi-adult.

2. **Your major doesn't much matter.** You will be surprised how infrequently

JOBDIG RECOMMENDS: www.swensonturner.com

you get asked about your major, so don't be all that shocked when your communications major background holds no water. Your GPA will count for something now, but no one will care really because it varies so much, school to school, major to major, etc. You think we don't know that?

3. **If you send out a resume, proofread it over and over and over.** Seriously. Can you spell? Make it easy for the employer to find you and contact you. Lose the studmuffin@gmail.com.

4. **If an employer happens to call you after you send out a resume, respond.** Here is the sad reality. Monster and all these BIG job boards have devalued your resume to the point, where you will send out hundreds of resumes and NOT get ONE reply. So, when you do get a reply, answer back. It will send a clear message to the company that there is a reason for them to acknowledge receiving your resume.

5. **Even if the job sounds terrible, interview anyway.** You should go on an interview a day, at least. Interview for the jobs you don't want, too. This is like asking the hottest girl at the bar for her myspace page, it keeps you in practice. Plus you don't make the shots you don't take as Michael Jordan used to say.

6. **Figure out the numbers.** How many phone calls to get one interview? Do that every day. How many interviews can you do per week, per day? How many companies have you actually called after you sent your resume? Your entire day should be devoted to finding this first, best job. The ratio of resumes to phone calls should be ONE.

7 . **Show your stuff.** Be prepared for each interview. You never know what might happen. Give yourself some positive self talk on the way to the interview, get there on time, early if possible. Come out of yourself. No one is going to see you in the hallway and say...YOU ARE THE ONE today, like some lottery winner, here is your employee badge.

8. **Go ahead and be a pest.** I used to say the applicant should follow up right to the point of becoming a pest to the HR person. Screw that. The chances of you actually becoming a pest are so remote, it is not even on the radar. Call back, write back, email back. Do it every other day, at least, until the company says "enough." But give them a new reason to like you on each of these contacts... "I was thinking about the job last night and had this idea..." or... "I forgot mention that I sold more Girl Scout cookies than anyone else..."

9. **Not sure of your passion quite yet?** It is easier to find your true calling once you have a job. Plus, you don't really know what you love, do you? I mean really? Those soap opera watching jobs are so hard to get anyway. Get started... finding what you don't like is even helpful. Practice showing some passion even if you are not in your keeper job.

JOBDIG RECOMMENDS: www.mediate.com

10. **Remember that almost any job is bigger than you are**. This is the secret of almost any job, and one that you can exploit. I don't care what the job... minimum wage to VP, I can tell story after story about some person who took this one job and made it into something more than the company thought possible. You know this happens...be that story and person. You will find your true passion faster with this attitude. Actually, learn to do this...and companies will find you. I promise.

Are You on a Career Path?

If there is one question I hear from Gen Y workers, it has to do with career paths...of wanting to understand how to pick a career, how to find passion and meaning in your life. Years ago, in my more smartass years, I would tell people that if you have to ask about your career path, chances are you aren't on it. For every person who has had a wonderful career, I think most will say it did not happen on purpose. Plus, people on the outside looking in, can help or sometimes advise. But really, it is up to you.

In my own case, I was not trained or educated to be an entrepreneur. But one day, Scott Drill was talking to me about his old company, Kroy, Inc., and how he believed they were making all these bad decisions. (He was 27 and I was 31 – the arrogance of youth is a powerful thing. But that is another topic.)

After hearing him talk about these mistakes and the size of the market, I asked a career and life changing question, with literally no preconceived thought. "Why don't we figure out how to make a product that does the same thing and compete against them." That simple unplanned question led to a lifelong relationship with Scott and has led to an entrepreneurial type career for me. We went ahead and formed a company to do just that.

James Michener, one of my favorite authors, didn't begin writing novels until he was forty years old. His books, *Hawaii, Centennial, Alaska* and several dozen more were all written after he turned forty. He said that anything you do before forty is simply practice. It might well take that long before you find your passion, or your calling in life.

So, my simple advice for Gen Y'ers who are concerned about finding your way, your calling, is to take comfort in the fact that it is ok to accumulate experiences, knowledge and awareness. You will find yours...just like Michener did. Sometimes the things you wait for and dream about, even if you don't know the specifics yet, will happen.

JOBDIG RECOMMENDS: www.firstepinc.com

Five Things You Can Do Now To Get a Better Job

Instead of dreaming about your career aspirations, – as in "if I only had my RN degree" – think in shorter time frames. What can you do next week, or start next week to get you a new job eventually? Here is my list for you to consider.

1. **Re-write your resume.** Create your resume from the employer's perspective. If you were the employer, why would you hire you? Chances are, you would eliminate a lot of it and concentrate on discussing how you would solve a specific problem for the employer. This naturally leads, then, to a process where you must find the company, understand their issues, and needs. Soon, you will determine that the old kind of resume is broken...and your new one will set you apart from other applicants.

2. **Find and start two new classes, typically available from your community ed department.** The first, is a speed reading course. There is nothing more valuable than increasing your reading speed and skills. The ability to read lots of materials will help you in numerous ways. The faster you read, the more you like to read. The more you read, the more you understand and the more you can do. The second class would be an accounting class. The language of business is accounting – understanding some basics will help you. Trust me.

3. **Enhance your current job.** The absolute best place to get a better job is simply to do better at your current one. Most jobs are bigger than the people who have them. What can you do to enhance your current job?

4. **Spend some time thinking about your own personal elevator pitch or story.** Learn how to best present yourself to others. Nearly every day, we are presented with an opportunity to share with someone...make your story memorable. A few days ago, I was in a business meeting with two people I knew, but they did not know each other. Near the end of the meeting, one of them said to the other,...this was completely out of the blue. "I know now about your business...tell me who you are," he asked. It was a revealing question and he got a surprising, insightful answer.

5. **Do something for someone else.** Get out of yourself a little. Your CAREER can be an overwhelming and all-encompassing issue. Maybe you can give someone else a bit of help too? We all need help and advice.

JOBDIG RECOMMENDS: www.bravenewworkshop.com

Please Don't Come To My Workplace, Mommy

If you are new in the workforce, chances are good that your parents are offering you advice, some of it wanted and most of it, not so. A decade or two of attending games and recitals, it is only natural for 'us' to be involved in your worklife. Some of us even call your bosses. You know, just to see what we can do for you. I kid you not. We live to embarrass you so you really have to be more direct with us.

I am offering you these suggestions for your Mom. Maybe this short list will get her to realize that you are in charge of your own life now. Cut and paste these five resolutions on a new piece of paper and scotch tape it to the fridge, right next to the "My 8th Grader is a Bright Star" certificate from 1996.

"Mom, I need you to –

1. **Chill out a bit.** I am not completely sure what I want to do with the rest of my life quite yet. I will figure it out. Just not by Friday. And tell Grandpa I am not going to med school.

2. **Not call the HR department.** I was only asking you for advice, there is no reason for you to call HR. I can do it, really.

3. **Not visit the office, every single week.** Really, I love you and yes, I am proud of you, too. But one visit to my office is enough, really. My co-workers think you are a stalker.

4. **Quit forwarding me all these self-help blog articles.** Most are pure BS, and they don't understand what I am going through anyway. I know you think they are clever. They aren't. Plus, my cubicle partner reads my emails over my shoulder and gives me grief.

5. **Not attend the company softball games**. Mostly, I am playing just to drink beer and hang out (pick up girls). This is not high school, you don't have to come watch me play co-ed softball."

JOBDIG RECOMMENDS: www.jhacareers.com

Chapter 3:

How to master the interview

Two Counter-Intuitive Strategies to Get You an Interview

I have heard job seekers tell me the following things as if they were fact:

"I saw the job opening online and sent my resume in. I am sure they will call me once they see my resume." And, "I had a good first interview. Even though it has been several weeks, they did say they would call me back."

Two things to remember:

1. **Be pro-active.** There are so many resumes floating around now because it is SO easy to send them, that the resume has become de-valued. If you want the job, do some research, do an informational interview at the company if you can, call the HR department or the department hiring. Do anything, something to get noticed. Your resume alone will not do it. Take charge of your job search.

2. **It is OK for you to call them.** I know someone who actually makes a point of screening candidates by seeing which one wants the job badly enough to call back, even though he says that he will call them. We all want to be wanted, and companies are no different. Show the company that you want to be part of it.

Before the Interview, Use Google

Before showing up at the interview, Google the company and the person you are interviewing. It only makes sense.

If you want to really impress the interviewer come prepared to ask questions about the company and the interviewer. If the interviewer blogs, read the blogs Find any company oriented blogs via technorati or bloglines, read them. Often the blogs will give you some official and not-so-official insights into the company.

Find the interviewer on Ryze, LinkedIn, Facebook, MySpace, ZoomInfo or almost any other social networking site. If you have time, search by company name on those sites and discover what other employees are thinking or saying about the company. Your task is to be better prepared for your interview and you should use any open and legal source to do so.

JOBDIG RECOMMENDS: www.findtheperfectjob.com

Lastly, don't weird out the interviewer by your in-depth knowledge. Don't mention his or her family or the latest round of layoffs. Find three or four areas of the business that interest you....and that you can positively impact if hired...and talk or ask about those areas.

The interviewer wants to know a couple of things:

Do I think this person will fit in?

How will this person help us?

It's your job to demonstrate both during the interview.

How To Start the Job Interview

Over 58%* of jobs are lost BEFORE the actual interview takes place. Yet advice-givers go on and on about the job interview itself, — how to respond to different questions, what the interviewer is trying to find out about you, etc. Fact is, before you sit down for the interview, you have already made your first impression, at the company. And no matter how well you do in the interview, you are either going uphill or downhill with the interviewer. Why not make sure you start out on a positive note? It is simple to do.

First, dress appropriately. This does not mean that you wear your Sunday-best, but it does mean that you wear neat, clean, pressed clothes that match the job level, and up one. If you are trying to get a job as a fork lift driver, you don't need to wear a suit. But, if jeans are the normal 'uniform' do NOT wear jeans, wear nice casual trousers, khakis for example. That is what I mean by 'up one.' If you are applying for an office job, and it is obvious that the office attire is business casual, you interview in a suit.

Next, get positive. Sure, you have been on interviews that have gone nowhere. But this one is THE one. There are all kinds of techniques to get yourself to this place. Read a positive article, talk with a mentor, listen to tapes, or convince yourself that this is THE opportunity you have been searching for.

Your biggest asset, smile. I know getting a job is stressful, and the interview itself is the most punishing aspect of it. But if you walk into the company without a smile on your face, and the resulting bounce in your step, you are digging yourself into a hole.

87% of all statistics are made up.   JOBDIG RECOMMENDS: www.juliejansen.net

How to greet people. I have seen many job seekers flunk common sense. The person you first meet when you get to the company will FOR SURE seek out your interviewer and comment on how you first made contact. Why wouldn't they? They care about their workplace environment and they want to make sure that new hires 'fit.' Get a smile on your face, make eye contact, offer a greeting, say clearly why you are here, and slowly say your name. Get their name too! I am not suggesting that you be insincere, just say something like "Hello, gosh it is nice outside today, isn't it? I am here to meet with Joe Smith about a job, my name is Sandy Jones." If the person does not offer their name, ask for it! You might need it later.

Assuming you have to wait for the interviewer, now is the right time to do your last minute informational interview. The person you just met can actually help you. Find out about the company, and what has happened recently. Something as simple as "Is there any news in the last week or so about the company? Anything exciting happen? I like what I know so far about your company, it looks like a great place." Most people will give a nice short answer to this question-comment…an answer that you can use in the interview. More than that, you will have established yourself as a positive person, and a person who is comfortable with others, and a person who is engaged enough to want to learn more about this company.

If you are offered coffee or a drink, take it. This might be counter-intuitive, but here is my reasoning. In sales, we know that if the prospect does some work in the sales process like sending in the requirements for the job, that is a sure sign that you are heading down the right path. So, in the job interview, if you are asked if you want coffee, this is a good sign. Key: do not accept it like he or she is your servant. Say something like "That would be nice. May I get it myself? Or come with you?" This is a great way to ask more questions about the company, or about this person. If you can make a connection to this person, you are starting to win the job.

The introduction to the job interviewer is important. I know you are nervous. We are all nervous on the first interview. This is where you must practice, this is a small detail that requires ten minutes of planning and practice. Your job interview has started and this might be the only part of it under your complete control. Why not get it completely right? I do not mean memorize some clever lines to give to the person, but practice sitting down, and then standing, extending your hand and making a good first impression. It is actually quite simple. "Hi, Mr. Jones, I am Sandy Jones. It is nice to meet you." It is NOT what you say it is all about how you say it. Talk with confidence and say it clearly. Make sure your handshake is business like and be ready to respond to any greeting that comes back to you. This is where you practice and think, think, think. What will he most likely say? He will ask if you found the location easily enough, he might make a comment on the traffic, or did you get coffee, you know the typical

JOBDIG RECOMMENDS: www.streetsmartjobsearch.com

responses. How will you answer them? Make sure your answers are clear, crisp and friendly. If you have the chance, make a comment about Ms. Smith, the receptionist, "Ms. Smith is sure a nice person, she represents your company well."

The walk to the interview room is also important. Who cares? you ask. Interviewers care. I know of an interviewer who literally watches to see how the candidate walks. If the person is sure and confident, he says, he can tell by how the person walks..it is almost like they have a bounce to their step. Certainly, they exude a positive, confident attitude. If they shuffle back to the conference room, that is a clear and bad sign.

Greet people you pass. You don't have to be a glad-hander here, doing something completely out of character. But if you pass people in the hallway, make eye contact (showing confidence) and a simple and appropriate greeting of, "Hi, how are you," is fine.

In the interview room or area, wait until your interviewer is seated first. Then you take your seat, and as soon as you sit down, move the chair slightly toward the interviewer, or at least lean forward. I have seen too many candidates sit down comfortably, and almost slouch into the seat. Your seated posture is as important as your posture during the walk back to the interview. Sit up straight, look attentive, lean forward, and make eye contact.

I know some people recommend looking around and making small talk…"I see you are a golfer." I don't think you should do that since it is so easy and superficial. Chances are your interviewer will make a bit of small talk at this point, be prepared. This is a simple conversation, it is like you are at a party and meet someone for the first time, it is not a big deal. The important thing is to be naturally curious, ask questions…but do that effectively, and listen and listen hard to the answer. Some job candidates lose it right here, they fail to make eye contact and give the impression that they are not truly listening. The best advice of all for this pre-interview stage is to listen up.

Now you are ready for the job interview. Good Luck.

When Can You Start?

There are only three good answers to this interview question.

1. As soon as I give proper notice to my current employer.

2. When would you like for me to start?

3. Right now.

JOBDIG RECOMMENDS: www.kenmooreassociates.com

The Winning Job Interview

The job interview is misnamed. Too many candidates think about the job interview in those terms—they think that the hiring manager person is going to ask me a bunch of questions and if I answer the questions correctly I may get the job.

What is really happening in the interview is actually quite simple. There are only two questions in the mind of the interviewer:

1. Do I like this candidate?

2. How can this person impact my dept/company – can they do the job?

Most of the interviewer's questions are designed to help them find out the answers to these two questions. Smart candidates, on the other hand, will use every tool at their disposal to serve up the answers at every opportunity.

For example, if every job candidate through research and informational interviews would find out more about the company and what they do, they could be better prepared to come into the interview armed with a HERE IS EXACTLY HOW I CAN HELP YOUR COMPANY plan, documented with ideas and action steps. All it takes is a bit of work, and some presentation skills.

Same idea with the bigger question of DO I LIKE THIS CANDIDATE? However, even this is in the control of the candidate. I am not suggesting undertaking a personality transplant, but I am suggesting that you think a bit about how to come across in a more likeable manner during the interview.

Humans tell stories. We have since the first caveman told Thor where all the bears were hiding and how to make fire (again). What is your story?

I suggest you prepare a short elevator pitch a 30-second summary on several topics that are sure to come up during the interview. Then when the interviewer asks a question, then, you are prepared with a story to tell that answers the question, sure, but is told in a compelling, interesting manner.

Let's say the interviewer asks you "Do you have any experience working with outside contractors?" The average candidate says, "Yes, at my last company we worked with XYZ company, and I was in daily meetings with them, presenting our changing issues." Good enough.

Or the candidate, having done some research and knowing that this job does work with outside contractors, but mindful of the always present DO I LIKE

JOBDIG RECOMMENDS: www.amazeyourself.net

THIS CANDIDATE question—prepares another answer:

"Yes, I have. (leaning in, because visual cues help) But, you know, I really have never thought of them as outside contractors. To me they have always been part of the company, because they are that critical to most companies' success. They are insiders, at least to me. For example, we had a high level project due on Monday and on Friday, a key spec was changed. I don't need to tell you what that can do to weeks, even months of planning and work. I was able to call our outsiders-insiders in over a weekend to help us get the job finished, on time. Frankly, I think our work surprised everyone. It wasn't me, even though I got the credit, it was my outside team."

Sure, the story is longer. It might take you more work to prepare, and prepare you must. So much of it has to do with not only the words, but your manner in telling it. Some hints to make you more likeable as you prepare the story—see if you can find them in the above example.

Hint 1: Make it more compelling by looking at the issue from a different angle. Maybe the interviewer has never thought of the issue in those terms.

Hint 2: Relate it to a real world situation for the interviewer. Make it real, be specific, not general.

Hint 3: Be humble.

Hint 4: Get engaged about your story. Practice it. Smile. Lean in. Think literally about how would Tom Cruise tell this story to make the audience believe it.

Body Language During the Job Interview

As interviewers, we pick up on a lot of things. How you sit during the interview. Even how you walk to the office ahead of us, do you have a bounce to your step or do you just shuffle along. It is all important.

Some people have a built in manner about them, that is either positive or negative. If you sense that you are starting interviews at negative-neutral, you might have negative body language. Why start the interview with Strike One already called against you? How can you really tell? Maybe a friend can be honest with you if you ask them.

JOBDIG RECOMMENDS: www.thesimplejobsearch.com

Three Types of Interview Questions and How to Handle Them

It is easy to find sample interview questions from hiring managers. For those who are very ambitious, you can even buy the same book that HR managers probably have on their bookshelf, *How To Ask Interview Questions*.

Typically, the problem is not with the questions, it's with your answers. And, even more to the point, it is being able to recognize a clear shift in the types of questions being asked.

In its simplest form, there are three stages to the interview and you have to pass through each stage. Think of the successive stages as gates that you have to open successfully. Only after you get through the last gate, do you get the offer.

Gate 1. Who are you? What have you done? Tell me about your background. You know all these questions, and hopefully, your answers by now. Some helpful pointers as you prepare for these type of questions: what the interviewer really wants to know is. Do I like this person? Does he/she fit in our company? So, remember it's not just about the answers, it is about your attitude. Make great eye contact. Use stories to showcase your skills. Frame your skills properly by using a story about how it solved a company problem. If you have passed thru this gate, you can almost feel the atmosphere change. It will become less awkward, more friendly.

Gate 2. Do you have any questions about our company? Let me tell you about our company (us) now. This gate is all about preparation and listening. First, prepare by doing your own research into the company. Read everything you can about the company. Find if there are company bloggers, do whatever you can to gain some insights about the company. The mood has changed, and probably to your advantage. The HR manager is now trying to sell you on their company. So, listen up. If you listen, the HR manager will tell you exactly what you need to do to seal the deal. Here is when you take out your note pad and take notes. Keep track of the issues, concerns, problems and other comments. I have seen people actually keep count of the times a certain issue was raised. If the hiring manager mentions the same challenge three times, do you think it is a major deal? Of course it is. Take notes, listen...and ask appropriate questions. All the time, be sure to bring up how your skills can contribute to solving the issue.

Gate 3. How do you like to work? Here is our benefits package. Here are the specific issues we need solved. Or, I hear you are a great softball player? These are all buying signals from the hiring manager. You have the job IF you don't

JOBDIG RECOMMENDS: www.anexpertresume.com

screw it up. Ask questions, be very polite and gracious. Clarify, clarify. If you don't understand something, now is the time to ask. Now is not the time to argue about the benefits package or negotiate. Now is the time to get the offer or to get agreement on exactly the next steps you must take.

Four Gutsy Things To Say on Your Job Interview

1. I'd like to explain why I'm absolutely the best applicant you've seen yet.

2. I have been preparing my entire life for this job.

3. I think I know what your biggest problem is right this instant – and I know I can solve it.

4. Instead of asking me about my past jobs, let's talk instead about how I would go about helping you, starting right now.

What To Say At the Job Interview, No Matter What the Job

Often job seekers want to know EXACTLY what to say during the interview. They hope there is a magic answer that results in "Ah, Miss Jones, you answered that one correctly…here's your job." Sorry, it does not work quite that easily.

There are some things you CAN say at every interview that WILL make you stand out from the other candidates. Here are a few of them.

1. **Please and thank you.** Mom was right. Interviewers notice this, I kid you not. Thank the person for the interview, for the coffee, for opening the door, and for granting you the interview after it's over. Do not worry about too many thank you's or pleases.

2. **Say something like, "I have been thinking about your company, and how I can make a contribution,"** and then proceed to enlighten the interviewer

JOBDIG RECOMMENDS: www.salesarchitect.com

on how you can help them. If you cannot do this, go back to square one, do some basic research and get to a point where you can say this....and, be believable. It does not make any difference if your analysis is wrong by the way. They do not expect you to come up with a solution to a big problem...it is enough that you were thinking about their company, in advance of the interview.

3. **Find something to compliment about the company.** This is easy. Did you like the way you were greeted at reception? Do people seem nice? Find something positive to say to the interviewer. Be genuine.

4. **Ask for the job.** Too many interviews end in no-man's land. Find out if they are interested by simply asking for the job. Too many interviews end with no real action...find out what you have to do next. This is clearly the most important thing you can say during the interview: "May I start right away?"

5. **Repeat what the interviewer says are the next steps are for you.** You will be told what the next steps are...repeat them back to the interviewer. I can't tell you how many people we have interviewed here, and the standard ending comment of our main interviewer is, "Well, how about if you think about the job, and if you are still interested give me a call by Friday, at 3 pm." He is very specific as to when he wants to be called back. You would not believe how many people do not hear this, or choose to forget it. I think they believe that if the company is interested, that we will take action and call back. We won't and neither will most companies.

It's Not the Job, Stupid. It's the Stupid Job.

Sometimes we do get what we wish for. Just make sure the job you get is one that you want. You can find out a lot about the job in the job interview. Here is one fact a lot of us forget about the job interview. You are interviewing them too!

Getting an offer might be the biggest sale you have ever made, but make sure it is a sale that you actually want. It is permissible for you to ask questions too. Find out the answers to questions that are important to you. Now is a perfect time to ask these questions. Think not what would Dad say, but what would Dad ask? Ask those questions.

JOBDIG RECOMMENDS: www.keepingthepeople.com

Walk around the company with the interviewer. Are people friendly? Can you sense the culture? Are people are interacting with each other and with you, a visitor?

Would you be proud to work there? Be sensitive to all that you see and hear. Trust your instincts and judgments.

Recently, I visited a company with about a thousand employees. It was a very modern office building and manufacturing facility. I could have been in the CIA building—it was incredibly quiet and had no energy. No fun at all. By next Tuesday, I would have been slitting my wrists, it was that boring. My host, a friend of mine, admitted it too. No fun. Yikes.

So make sure the job you get, is the job you want. You can tell even during an interview.

Three Job Candidates to Remember

As I look back on my career, I have interviewed lots of candidates and applicants for jobs. I was thinking back on what any of them had said that stood out. I think there are about ten applicants that answered a question in such a way that even now, years later, I can remember how they answered. Here's why I remembered just three of them.

Candidate One. My company was interviewing for sales reps with experience. Each candidate had good experiences with good companies, and all appeared to have similar, successful backgrounds. Except for one.

His resume seemed average, but it lacked sales experience. For some reason, however, I invited him to be interviewed. Perhaps it was how polished and professional his resume looked. I can't remember the details about why I called this person in for an interview.

When he arrived at my office, he was very nice appearing, sharp, and wanted to get into sales, although he had, up to that point, not worked in sales at any point in his career. He thought it would give him some career advantages and he genuinely believed he could do it and that he would be able to learn quickly. Despite his conviction, we were looking for sales people with prior experience so as a final gesture, I asked him if he had any sales experience at all anywhere in his past. Maybe he had sold Christmas cards, door to door.

He stopped for a minute and then said, "No, I come from a very small town, there were only about fifty kids in my high school class. No one really sold Christmas cards, our parents and relatives just bought them, I didn't really sell them." I liked this answer a lot, but he continued, "but, at my high school, homecoming was a huge deal. The most popular and prettiest girl was always the homecoming queen. In my senior year, the girl was unbelievably pretty, smart, popular, and every guy wanted to date her. I think I can sell something because I married her."

The point is, there is always something in your background that you can make applicable to almost any job.

Candidate 2. This applicant was very highly regarded and did well during the entire interview. I was close to recommending that she advance to the next round of interviews when she made a comment that cemented the deal.

What's more, she said, "I will never ask for a raise."

This comment obviously took me by surprise, so I asked why.

"I will work so hard for you and do so much more than you expect, that I know you will see that and provide as many future opportunities as you can inside the company for me. I won't ever have to ask."

The point is, she showed confidence in herself and was willing to demonstrate it.

Candidate 3. I once had an interview with a candidate for an Administrative Assistant. The conversation was almost over when, reaching for one last pertinent question, I asked if there were something else about her that I should know that she was particularly proud of being able to do.

She replied, "Yes, there is one thing. I am always honest and will never lie to you, even if and when I make a mistake. This does not mean that I am brutally honest and make rude, blunt comments about your suits and ties, but when you ask me if something has been done or the current status of a project I am working on, you will always get the truth."

I wish more candidates had this strength. There is nothing more valuable than this sort of reputation in the minds of your co-workers, management, partners, and customers.

The "When Can You Start?" Question and What to Say Next

If the interview goes well, and the interviewer asks. "When can you start?" what is the best way to handle this question? It depends on the situation.

Situation 1. They have made you an offer, the job and the compensation plan are to your liking. But you are helping out at a volunteer agency that really needs your help for about a month longer. You are afraid the new company will want you to start sooner.

As always, honesty is the best policy and should govern all that you do. If you have made a commitment, it is best to keep your commitment. I would recommend discussing it with both the new company and the volunteer agency. Perhaps you could work part-time, for both or either. The key issue for you is to do your best to keep the job offer while maintaining your own personal commitments. Most companies have a little bit of flexibility for the right person and will make some adjustments. This is one of those worrisome situations that might cause a sleepless night or two...but just think it through and be open and honest.

Situation 2. They have not yet made you an offer. You are currently working and feel like you must give at least two weeks' notice to your employer.

This one is more typical and fairly simple. You can simply say that assuming we are in agreement here, I can give my current employer two weeks' notice, so my start date will be..... If the company says they want you to start sooner, the best way to handle this is to say that you would be happy to see if your current employer will allow you to leave sooner...but that the decision should be theirs. You are more than willing to do what you can on your off time to get started.

Situation 3. You are not currently working.

Also simple. Just let them know that you are ready and willing to begin as soon as they are ready for you.

How to Un-Bore Yourself

Some people live their entire work lives like this, bored silly. We can fight against boredom in our work life...but it really starts in the initial job interview. Far too many of us, bore the interviewers...and ourselves.

When you are in the middle of a job interview, do you find yourself thinking... "Boy, I am not coming across as my normal self. I am boring the interviewer."

This happens to all of us sometimes. Typically, it is due to nerves, and being so committed to doing a good job in the interview, that you forget to be natural.

So, how can you fight against this? Interviewers want people who are not boring. They need to be energized too. They are looking for candidates who demonstrate that they are special, and will offer something unique to the workplace. Here are a few things you can do to come across better during the interview:

1. **Tell stories.** Find three stories of about one minute length that happened to you in your personal life. This is some noteworthy event, maybe it is a story that is told about you at family gatherings. And then, figure out how to tie it to the workplace. A simple transition just takes a bit of brainstorming..."I see that you make famous red, white and blue widgets here. That reminds of when I was a kid and ….." I know this sounds hokey, but it always works. People love to hear stories, and the more personal the better.

2. **Use analogies and metaphors.** Look some up on the internet. Find unusual combinations, and practice them. Interviewing at Winnebago? Start smiling and say something like..."Your company reminds me of a saying my dad always used: 'You can't clean the garage with the Winnebago parked in there.' I never thought I would get to meet the people AT Winnebago."

3. **Read something inspirational right before you interview.** Use positive self talk to get your energy up. Have you watched a football movie? Locker room speeches? Do you have any doubt that those work? Make your locker room speech, and then give it to yourself.

4. **Practice.** Practice interviewing using these techniques and get interviews for jobs you don't really want, just to practice the ideas here. Why wait for that BIG interview to try a new approach. It is a legal thing to practice in a real life situation.

5. **Above all, remember that you must show that you can do their job.** Do your research on the company and the job. Come prepared. The preparation alone will give you a new-found confidence which will show through during the interview.

JOBDIG RECOMMENDS: www.emergeinternational.com

Eats, Shoots & Leaves: Do You Need a Personal Elevator Pitch as a Jobseeker?

The answer is yes. But first a clever story:

A panda walks into a bar, orders and eats a meal, pulls out a six-shooter, fires it into the air, and starts to walk out. The puzzled waiter looks at him and asks, 'Why?' The panda throws a poorly punctuated dictionary on the table and says, 'I'm a panda. Look it up. The waiter finds the definition and reads, 'Panda: Large black and white mammal, indigenous to China. Food source: eats, shoots, and leaves.'"

Lynn Truss could have called her book, *The Proper Guide to Punctuation* but it does not have the same impact as her chosen title *Eats, Shoots & Leaves*, her wildly popular punctuation guide.

Most job seekers make the same mistake. When asked to tell something about themselves, instead of creating a memorable statement about who they are, what they might be able to bring a company, they flounder like a dying mackerel on the dock, mumble, mumble, mumble...er, er, um...well, I am yadayadayada.

Take some time to craft a 30-second elevator pitch about yourself just for these situations. And remember the famous words of Jerry Garcia:

"It's not enough to be the best at what you do; you must be perceived as the only one who does what you do."

You are a unique jobseeker with unique talents. Craft your own personal pitch to become more memorable and less forgettable.

JOBDIG RECOMMENDS: www.drloisfrankel.com

The Interview is Over, Not

From time to time, someone will bring a job candidate by my office to be introduced. I am supposed to do the typical meet and greet deal, which I dutifully do.

I have rarely met a job candidate that handled this situation gracefully. I generally get a "nice to meet you" mumble, mumble, mumble, an Ozzy Osbourne type response.

These chance meetings are CRUCIAL for a job candidate. Yet, most fail due to lack of planning. Or, they believe the job interview is over—and are trying their best to get out the door and have no time to be nice to some random person they just met.

At our company, we make sure all candidates meet some of their future co-workers. We look for how they interact with our current staff. One does NOT need to be a hiring guru to pick out the best candidates by just observing them as they walk around and meet people.

Realize that the interview is not over, until you are out of sight. I have heard about interviewers who walk the candidate to their car just to see inside the car. They are looking for neatness and no beer cans in the backseat.

The Class Everyone Thought You Took, But You Didn't

Most of the time, the condescending tone of the career pundits bugs me. It's always "Sally, you idiot, here are the mistakes on your resume." Or, "Billy Bob, here is how to answer these typical interview questions."

But I thought you knew better. Come to find out there are a lot...I mean a LOT... of job seekers who are clueless about the basics, of how a business operates and recruits. This is INTERVIEWING 101: THE CLASS EVERYONE THOUGHT YOU TOOK, BUT YOU DIDN'T. It's a lecture. Please pardon my bluntness, but some of your friends, NOT YOU, need this direct approach.

1. When you send out a resume, send a cover letter too. Make both perfect.

2. Keep track of what company and to whom you send your resume and

JOBDIG RECOMMENDS: www.mbrownassociates.com

cover letter. You do this so when you are called by the company's recruiter, you don't say things like, "How did you get my resume," or "who are you and why are you calling me?"

3. **Google each company.** Read and remember just a little bit about the company. This is so when you are called for the initial interview you are NOT completely in the dark about the company. You want to avoid comments like, "Mmmm, I have never heard about your company, what do you do?"

4. **Before the interview, study more about the company.** Granted, this is a lot like homework. Find out as much as you can about the company and industry. What do they do? What else can you find out about them?

5. **Arrive early for the interview.** If necessary, scout it out beforehand. Dress appropriately. The easy rule is to dress one level up from the normal workplace attire for the business. If you are a guy and you have found it is business casual during the workday, wear a tie. Simple.

6. **Everyone you meet is important.** Quick story: I know a young guy who was being interviewed by a large health care company here in Minneapolis. The woman who took him back to the interview area was like Hilda the Hun, came across almost mean-spirited. The young guy treated her nicely and made small talk. She then went out of her way to make sure he was interviewed first, and even gave him a tip on how to handle the interviewer, her boss.

7. **Make eye contact and have a bounce in your step.** I can't tell you how many people shuffle, eyes-down on the way to and from the interview, and the small talk is a series of near-grunts, "Yep, nope, ummm." Act interested, engaged and a bit vibrant. Attitude trumps most skills in this first setting.

8. **Use your manners.** Take notes during the interview. Ask questions. Be nice.

9. **After the interview, send a note to the interviewer**. We have interviewed over 200 recent graduates for some sales positions. Guess how many sent a follow up note? One. 1. No kidding.

10. **After about a week, make contact again, via email and with a call.** If you are smart, you will have sent a note to the person who took you back to the interview, too. Remember the young guy who met Hilda the Hun? Well, he sent her a note. On his subsequent interview, he met her again. Here is what he said, "She was so happy to see me, I thought she was going to kiss me in the reception area. As we walked past her desk, I noticed on her desk that she had a picture of her kids, her dogs and then my note was propped up against one of them." Is there any wonder he got the offer?

Class dismissed.

JOBDIG RECOMMENDS: www.martynemko.com

Yogi Berra, JobSeeker

What's the first thing that comes to mind when you hear the name "Yogi Berra?"

Admit it – it was most definitely NOT that he was perhaps the greatest catcher in baseball history, or that he held baseball records for almost thirty years, but you thought of all his famous quotes. They are even called by their own word: Yogisms.

After an amazing baseball career, it's almost sad that we remember him not for catching almost 100 World Series games, or being a world champion ten times, or fielding 1,000% for an entire season, but for his mangling of the English language with quotes like: "This is like deja vu, all over again." Or, "You can observe a lot just by watching." Or, "baseball is 90% mental, the other half is physical." Or, maybe even, "Nobody goes there any more, it's too crowded."

Funny. And, the more he talked, the funnier he got. I see the same thing happening with job seekers, especially during initial interviews. The more they talk, the funnier they get.

So, words to the wise, pay attention to what you are saying. This is not the time to "shoot the breeze" with the interviewer. I don't care if they do seem all friendly and "cool." Almost everything you say will be judged and re-played. I have heard interviews played back almost verbatim between interviewer and hiring manager, long after the applicant has left the building. "I asked this, and she said this," sort of thing. Words do matter.

The winning interviews are natural, sure. Please realize it is permissible, even legal, for you to practice the interview, how and what you are going to say. Learn to tell a story about how you can bring value to the company, using your own background or experience. Tell it in an engaging way in two minutes...can you do that?

Give me an applicant who knows how to start off with this statement – "I have been doing some research into your company and here is how I can help..." – and if what comes next is engaging, interesting, on point and is delivered well, chances are pretty good they will be in our lineup.

Don't find yourself saying later, as Yogi was quoted, "I really didn't say everything I said."

JOBDIG RECOMMENDS: www.maryelizabethbradford.com

Chapter 4:

Attitude determines altitude

Standard Responses to Any Boss Question

The other day I was reminded of Don Carmen, the major league pitcher who answered a reporter once, "They don't pay me to hit" when he was asked about his lack of hitting.

Carmen went on to quasi-baseball fame by posting a list of his standard answers on his locker to any future questions by, "Stupid reporters." Reporters could simply pick from his list: "I'd rather be lucky than good." Or "we're going to take the season one game at a time." Or "We'll get them tomorrow."

So, with apologies to Carman, I thought I would provide some canned answers for you to use in the workplace…you know, for when your boss comes by and asks you something difficult.

1. That's not my job.
2. But my MySpace page helps me stay in touch with the culture.
3. You can't monitor my emails.
4. We have to make a profit.
5. **Let's automate everything that has to do with the customer.** It will make them happy.
6. I understand our customer.
7. **Let's be careful and make only small, incremental changes.** Anything else is too risky.
8. Just tell me what you want me to do and I will do it.
9. **Really?** No one told me.
10. **1970: I have to do some research at the Library.** In 1990 it was: My kid has a soccer game. In 2000: I have a doctor's appointment. 2008: What's it to you?

JOBDIG RECOMMENDS: www.workingresources.com

Lessons from Famous Movies: Apollo 13

Remember the scene when the disaster is looming and it is looking awfully grim at NASA? Someone then says, "This could be the biggest disaster in NASA history."

Gene Kranz, the mission director in Houston, who is being played by Ed Harris, stands up straight in the midst of all the turmoil and says, "I believe that this will be the finest moment in NASA history."

There is most always a silver lining in every cloud that comes your way. And those who understand that and can rally people even during the darkest or toughest times nearly always win. Or, as someone once told me…" If you get the reputation of making chicken salad out of chickenshit, you will be ok."

The YeahButs Have Arrived

One of my core beliefs is that some people have a built-in system for dealing with yeahbutt-itis. Yeahbut-itis is the God-given ability to come up with all kinds of reasons NOT to do something.

Whether it is changing careers, finding the right college or even how to make a presentation to your boss, we all can conjure up Yeahbuts.

"Yeah, but if I do it this way, this might happen."

"Yeah, but if I go to Harvard, I won't be able to see Susie on weekends."

"Yeah, but if I go to med school, what happens if I don't make it?"

"Yeah, but if I don't get the promotion, what will dad think about me?"

Need some more? Think back on almost every decision you ever, I mean EVER, made and admit that you did have some YEAHBUTS in your mind, convincing you to take the easier path.

Your ability to handle these yeahbuts says a lot about how successful your life will be.

JOBDIG RECOMMENDS: www.halleland.com

How To Walk Your Talk

Susan Heathfield, a management consultant, wrote about how one should walk your talk as it applies to encouraging change and continuous improvement in the workplace.

Susan has some good ideas—model the behavior you want, follow the rules, be a part of the team, help others achieve their goals, do what you say you are going to do, hold strategy and communication meetings and ask senior managers to police themselves—all good stuff. Mom and apple pie.

Yet, something is missing. I am sure that the upper, non-ethics based management at Enron believed in all this. Yet,—

I am also sure that the CEO's who benefit from the me-me-me-me stock options awards, believe in all this. Yet—

I am also sure that every noteworthy and famous person who is in the public eye but who has had a very visible, embarrassing fall, like Hugh (she's a hooker?) Grant or Bill Clinton, also believed in all this. Yet—

I am left wondering if it is so simple, so dependent on rules, RULES, why do we keep seeing leaders who do not walk THEIR talk. Why don't they just follow the rules? There must be something more.

In thinking back over my career, the leaders who have consistently 'walked their talk' in every area of their life, have been exceptionally humble and modest. "Walking their talk" never actually occurs to them–it is a natural thing. Even the phrase seems contrived, made up. We should be talking about character-based leadership, instead.

So, can we teach leaders to do this? I am not so sure.

Learn from your Mistakes

Most new companies will admit that it is not what they started with that matters, it is what they ended up with. In short, product development is a series of making mistakes, correcting them and making the mousetrap better. So is career development. And, since

JOBDIG RECOMMENDS: www.distinctiveweb.com

it is your career, you have the power to fix it.

I once attended a talk by one well known entrepreneur who actually said, in the way of advice, that he recommended going bankrupt at least twice so that you can understand the pain, and success, associated with failure. That was stupid advice—but there is some truth in the fact that we all do learn life lessons from our failures. You must have some things in your career that you know, deep down, that are holding you back.

So, if you can admit this is true, how can you learn from these "failures?"

Simple. It might be time to have a real heart-to-heart talk with yourself. What are the reasons you are in your current spot? Let's assume for a minute, and this is a big assumption here: That your 'spot' is completely due to your own attitude and performance. Work with me here.

Make a list of those attributes that you know you need to change. You know what they are, don't kid yourself. Make a similar list of the solutions under your control. Don't make this list long or complicated.

Think small things first. Make small and incremental improvements in those areas of development completely under your own control. Don't worry about changing the world quite yet.

Your list should look like this, in two columns write: **Things to work on** and **What I am going to do, exactly.** Every day, look at your list. Add and subtract items.

Taking a Step Back

Many times in your career it is necessary to take a step backward, either in salary or position, in order to get on a faster track.

The way to look at this is to consider the step back as an investment, something that will pay off to a greater degree in the future. This delayed gratification has worked for countless people, including most entrepreneurs I know, who have given up steady paychecks for a shot at their dream. The trick, I suppose, is to have a supportive family and an iron clad belief in your ability to make the 'investment' pay dividends.

JOBDIG RECOMMENDS: www.vitalwork.com

Learn to be an Innovator

This is a huge subject. Numerous books, seminars, and articles have been written about innovation. I don't pretend to be the be-all, end-all on the subject.

Here's the deal: Every business wants people who do their job well, with a good attitude. They also want good thinkers who 'innovate' to improve their job, department and company. Some people seem to have a tough time doing this, partly because they don't know how; finding that it is much easier to blame the environment, i.e. "I have great ideas but they don't listen to me." So, these people are frustrated and know they could contribute more.

Since all adults have ADD, I thought I would boil it down how you can become known as an innovator. Here is my 3-Step Plan:

1. Read constantly.

2. Always be thinking – How can I re-arrange old things in new ways?

3. Tell others about your idea(s). Share your ideas all the time, in good humor.

Money Saving Tips

Most of us want to make more money. Insightful.

Realize that money saved is like the same (only more) as making more money. I am constantly reminded of this at the local Starbucks. Why do I pay $4 when I know I can get coffee basically for free at my office? I have no good reason. If you make near the minimum wage now, one cup is an hour of work. After taxes, etc.

It's like Dilbert's Scott Adams said once, when asked in a grocery store why he bought the most expensive water on the shelf…. "If I'm dumb enough to buy water, I'm certainly dumb enough to pay too much for it!"

JOBDIG RECOMMENDS: www.workexposedblog.com

Simple Things

Simple things make my day. It surprises me that people at work forget the following:

When you pass someone in the hallway, smile and offer up a greeting.

When you get in an elevator and make eye contact, say hello.

When you approach a door at the same time as someone else, open it for them to pass through first.

When the coffee is almost out, go ahead and make some new…yourself.

And then, clean up the area…yourself.

Clean up the conference room after the meeting…yourself.

Talk more quietly on your cell phone. Or turn it off.

Say pleaseandthankyouandexcuseme more. That reminds me, do you want to hear my Elvis impersonation? "Thankyouverymuch, pass the peanut butter." Lip curl.

Get Happy For Others

This is really dad-advice now. Too many of us are concerned with OUR lives, OUR jobs, OUR problems, OUR plans, and OUR successes. Even with our loved ones we tend to be competitive. With co-workers it is even more so.

Try this approach. Instead of being quite so competitive and so quick to compare your successes with others, try instead to be genuinely happy for their success. Do it not because you have a hidden agenda or motive; in fact, do not expect anything in return. Someone calls this the emotional bank account, a sort of savings account of good wishes. I think the more you practice this attitude—something very positive will happen to and for you. But, again, you cannot fool anyone…you must give this out before it will come back to you. It may take a long time, even.

Very few people can do this.

Beware of People Who Want to Negotiate for You

No one cares as much as you do about your business or personal life.

Even if you think you need outside counsel/advice, realize that even the best professionals lose sight of getting the deal done...often they get too wrapped up in the process. Or, are too intent on winning the negotiation. Keep in mind that if they lose the deal, they have only lost a small fee whereas you have lost a lot more. This advice applies whether you are buying or selling a home or negotiating a business deal. Stay involved and engaged. No one understands your viewpoint as well as you do.

I know people who think that using outside professionals will get them a better deal or arrangement. Instead, the "professional" has completely screwed up the deal. Trouble is, his client will never understand that, because the professional has successfully inserted himself into the middle of what could be a great relationship between the principles. Sometimes professional advisors can help, but they can also lose you the deal.

What is absolutely the WORST are those 'professionals' who really aren't that accomplished, but who act like they are...they look good in a suit, and seem to know enough buzz words to get the gig.

Role Models Needed

"When people are free to do as they please, they usually imitate each other."
– *Eric Hoffer*

or,

"The surest predictor of success in your life is to see whom you hang with."
– *Dad*

JOBDIG RECOMMENDS: www.ekminspirations.com

I Work in a Small Company, Do I Have to Take Out the Trash?

Yes.

I hope that everyone pitches in and does this kind of work. I know it is not in your job description, but it most surely fits under, "Does what is needed to help us achieve our goals."

I realize that some of these things seemingly cross the line…such as picking up the owner's dry cleaning, babysitting her kids, or helping her clean her personal house.

I think in these cases you have to assume goodwill, and assume that somehow these activities will help the business. If only because it frees up the primary revenue producer from a mundane task that she has calculated can be best handled by you. You, are in effect, saving her time to do more, make more. In all likelihood, these 'sacrifices' will pay off for you.

In the meantime, swallow your pride a bit and do it all in good humor.

No One is 15% Smarter Than You

More than once, I have heard bright twentysomethings say something like "I am just not as smart as I should be. I feel so inadequate." This perhaps is a sure sign of insecurity.

I have a 15% rule—which basically goes like this: No one is more or less than 15% smarter or dumber than anyone else. (I know this is a generalization and there are exceptions to every rule!)

But it pretty much holds true in most companies. No one is head and shoulders over you in terms of pure IQ.

Like everything, it is what you choose to do with yours that matters most.

JOBDIG RECOMMENDS: www.tablegroup.com

Developing All Your Skills

John is my imaginary friend who is successful by most measures. He has a great job, makes a lot of money and has all the skills he needs to continue to climb the corporate ladder. He even has dreams, of someday, buying his own business. John has an MBA, but has added experience to that education…experience in real world jobs, with real pressures, and has performed at a very high level. His post-college mentor told him right after college, that advancement was contingent on his career skill development and on how he applied those learned skills. Seemingly, that advice has worked.

Then, why is John always in debt? Each year he makes more and more, yet he can't seem to get ahead. He is frustrated and worries too much. But he did exactly what he was supposed to do. Or did he? Back in the day, yes. But John has a problem that confronts each generation, and it might even be getting worse.

He does not understand his own personal financial life. Tragically, many people now in the workforce will face the same situation. No matter how successful you are in your career, you must pay attention to your own financial situation, your credit standing, your savings plan, and, even more important, your own spending plan.

If you don't come to grips with this part of your life NOW, you will continue to advance your own career, only to see any gains being wiped out by your own lack of attention and abilities. Now is the time to stop believing that doing better work and getting constant raises is all you need to get to financial heaven. I don't want to lecture you on what to do. You are a grown up, you figure it out. I am only saying that personal financial skills cannot be ignored. Do some studying now and get it right. Don't get started with bad habits.

Assume Goodwill

Far too many problems can be avoided if you assume goodwill on the part of the other person…FIRST.

Maybe this will lead to trouble…and I know there are evil people out there who want to do bad things to others…but mostly, we are a nation of good, quality people who want to do the right, nice and even moral thing. Don't lose sight of that.

JOBDIG RECOMMENDS: www.career-resumes.com

Mental Mentors

According to the Greeks, the goddess Athena liked to travel down to Earth, disguised as a man named "Mentor" to advise the young son of Ulysses. Similarly, mentors help guide and encourage younger people.

These mentors can encourage you, motivate you and, in general, inspire you to go to places you could not have traveled to alone.

Most of us know how to find mentors...whether a family friend, teacher, or a first boss. The usual approach is to ask the person, "Will you help me in my career? I would like to have someone to give me advice."

This is normal...and the hardest.

Instead, create mental mentors for yourself. The more, the merrier. Simply recognize attributes and characteristics that you like in people–someone who is calm when everyone else is in panic mode; someone who obviously likes and respects the worker at the bottom, someone who has a glass is always full outlook, someone who never swears, etc.

Then, resolve to be more like that person. Don't just admire them or say something like, "I wish I could be more like Jim or Jane." Create a vision of this person, and be specific...what they do, the attitudes, characteristics of that person,...and, start acting more like them.

I think this might be the best predictor of success for someone new to the workforce. A great interview question could be, "Tell me who your mentors are and what you have learned from them?"

Then, once you have become successful or have successfully modeled that behavior, be sure to tell that mental mentor that you have used them in this way. What a thrill that would bring, I am sure.

JOBDIG RECOMMENDS: www.jobhuntersbible.com

Beware of Experts

"Before I got married I had six theories about bringing up children; now I have six children and no theories."
– *John Wilmot, English Lord*

There are too many experts around with a lot of answers who have not actually tried their theories in real life situations. I understand that some people are advisors or teachers, or consultants. But I seem to learn more from those teachers and mentors who have had some practical world experience. Their lessons are more believable to me, and more relevant. Trouble is, some people who have not done much in the 'real' world have focused their energies and skill on their own line of pitter-patter, which all sounds good, really good–but does not help much, if at all. They can sell you a total line of BS. Most self-help business books fall into this category.

Two Kinds of Jobs. What are They?

Good and bad? Highly paid and not so highly paid? A job you love and a job you hate?

Increasingly I have come to believe that the last one is the best lens through which to view your job. This is why Richard Bolles' *What Color Is Your Parachute* counsels people to find their true passion in life and find work there. Unfortunately, too many people are stuck in the daily routine and reality of simply working for a paycheck at the end of the day. It is hard to find work that matches your passion if you are unsure of what your passion truly is.

A lot of it simply has to do with your own attitude about work and your own job. Some people would complain if you gave them dirty $100 bills, and I know a lot of people like to complain about their work. But it is so true that your attitude really does determine how successful you will be in your career. You absolutely can choose your own attitude. Every day when you wake up, barring extreme scenarios, you have the ability to decide if your day will be a good one or a rotten one. So work on your own attitude first. Chances are you will be in a better frame of mind to actually discover ways you can love your current job.

Your current job is the best job you have today. Make the most of it.

JOBDIG RECOMMENDS: www.emperform.com

Be Truthful

I am not sure where shading the truth got started, but it is certainly noticeable. I understand that oftentimes, telling the truth is the hardest thing to do. (insert small violin here)

But puh-lease, make honesty part of who you are. Once you get known as a truth teller, particularly to power, you have it made.

The things that I hear that really gripe me are excuses that are nothing but lies. I would much rather hear an honest but truthful explanation of why something is late, why you missed the meeting, or what someone said, etc. Do not think for a minute that your managers cannot tell when you are shading the truth. Maybe it will work for a while, even. But longterm, it won't and it will impact what people say about you, and your chances for promotion.

I am telling you we can tell who the truthful ones are, and which ones aren't. Be the former.

Sometimes Your Passion Finds You

Career advisors are often asked… "How do I find my passion?"' I'm no career advisor but I do have gray hair so I get asked that as well. Since no one pays me for this type of advice, I generally have a smartass answer like, "I think you can find passion at Deja Vu on Washington Avenue. Just be sure your shots are up to date."

Maybe the right answer is that your passion finds you. You don't find it. It sort of sneaks up on you when you least expect it, bites you in the ass, and says…"Here I am you nimrod, I am right here in front of you!"

I won't get to write too many career advice books with this as the theme, I know, I know.

JOBDIG RECOMMENDS: www.robinryan.com

How To Be Positive When Everyone Else Isn't

We all know that positive people are more interesting, more engaged, more fun to be around and more successful. Typically. Plus they get the prettiest girls.

Everyone has heard: Be positive, be positive, be positive.

The issue is not so much in understanding the 'be positive' outlook on life, we all get that. What we don't get often is how to MAKE ourselves positive when times or our own situation is bad. The life-changing skill you must learn is:

How to make yourself positive when you feel just the opposite.

I have a few tips:

The first is tried and true, although it does sound a bit too Zig Ziglar-ish for me too. Fake it til you make it. This does take some acting ability, no doubt, but it works. When you are feeling negative, make yourself act differently. Feel like hiding? Go out and meet someone new. In a bad mood? Call someone and act like a real sunshine pump over the phone. Even if you feel bad, act like you don't. This works.

Next, make a list of everything that is going right for you. Even if it is only ten items long...something is working for you. Strive to add to this list.

Realize that you feeling all negative is giving some hidden power over to the thing that just happened. Let's say you are driving home, and absentmindedly cut someone off in traffic. They flip you the "bird." You go instantly from singing along with your iPod to being out of sorts. The bird flipper did it to you. So now hours later, why are you allowing some jerk to still affect you? Move on. Don't give this kind of power over to someone.

Oh, and that brings me to the best comment I think I ever heard from a job applicant. I asked him for a skill he might have that was NOT on his resume. He said, "I can make chicken salad out of chickenshit." With one comment I knew he would make an outstanding hire.

Lastly, if you can give yourself positive and affirming self talks when you need them, you will do well. Only you can 'make' yourself positive.

JOBDIG RECOMMENDS: www.jobsearchhandbook.com

Get a Bad Job Before Your Good One Starts

Let's say you are about to attend your own graduation ceremony. You will soon hear all the be-all-you-can-be speeches, enough to last you quite a while. And, sure, congratulations, for your achievement is in order. So – congratulations! Now, what are you going to do?

Let's suppose you have a job but it starts in a month or two. Back when you interviewed, you thought it would be fun to have a few weeks off...you know, because the last few weeks of school were SOOOO hard. But now, Mom and Dad are on your case – it is fast becoming obvious to you that watching TV all summer before your grown up job starts will NOT be fun. Plus you are running out of money.

Go find the worst job you can. Something that involves labor, hard work and little pay. This is so you will be able to tell YOUR kids in the future that hard work made you what you are today – you did some of it back in the day and didn't want any more of it. Plus it will give you a bit of humility and a better understanding of just how lucky you are.

The 5% Rule

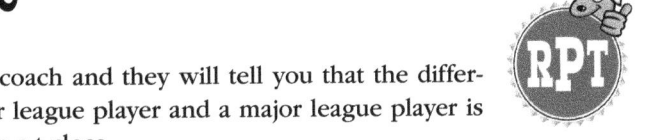

Ask any professional coach and they will tell you that the difference between a minor league player and a major league player is only about 5%. It is t-h-a-t close.

A friend of mine recently went through a week long executive coaching event, helping him add to his already impressive leadership skill set. He was reminded there that most of us already have the skills necessary to win or do better or enhance our skills...it is just a matter of fine tuning, tweaking that extra 5% so that we get to the big (ger) leagues.

Each of us has the ability to find that extra 5%. Keep in mind, this 5% rule does not apply if you are in T-ball...the differences between a T-Ball player and Barry Bonds are waaaaaay more than 5%. I am talking about the differences between individuals already with the requisite skills or similar jobs. I am just saying – you are closer than you think.

JOBDIG RECOMMENDS: www.shellyburke.net

How To Find a Mentor Mid Career

We tend to think of mentoring as something one does with someone younger. Young people, being all positive and energetic, want to find someone with more experience...wisdom, even...to help guide them during their career.

But there are plenty of 'older' workers who also would like a mentor. For whatever reason, they now understand that, "Oops, maybe I don't know everything I need to know here." Mentors can help all of us learn more, better and develop new skills.

Heard the saying, "You can't teach an old dog new tricks?" In my mind, old dogs need new tricks more than anyone else. So – how does someone mid-career find a mentor? Here are a few ideas:

1. **Ask someone for advice.** This might be the best advice ever given to me, actually. No one can refuse someone who asks for advice or help. I once observed a very low level manager meeting the chairman of one of the nation's largest bank holding companies, making idle chit chat, and then, after about 2 minutes, he said, "Would you mind if I called you to have coffee sometime? I would like to ask you for some career type advice." The Banker, who had his day fully scheduled in 15 minute blocks, said, "Sure, here is my cell phone, call me."

2. **Honestly, do a career assessment checkup.** I am not talking about having an assessment test. You have been in the workplace – you KNOW what you need to learn. Do you understand sales? How about bookkeeping or accounting? Can you program a simple website in HTML? All three of those can be learned with a mentor and mentors are easy to find. They are already in your company. Buy the sales manager coffee one day. Buy the IT guy a coffee too.

3. **Take a class, join a business club or organization.** These are traditional ways of getting out of your comfort zone, allowing you to interact with others from other companies and skill sets.

Above all...the trick to locating a mentor is quite easy: Find someone who knows something you don't and ask for their help.

JOBDIG RECOMMENDS: www.resourcemaximizer.com

Summer Doldrums and What to do About Them

It is nice outside, perfect even. People are out biking, hiking, golf and playing softball. There are barbq's, boats, and girls walking their dogs. And then, there's work.

If we lived in France, you would have the entire summer off. Ok, I am kidding, maybe half of it is all. Those French.

But you don't. You have to work, and every day too.

So, how can you motivate yourself, especially if you are relatively new to the workforce…and used to having summers off, just like those silly French? Here are a few ideas:

1. **Man up. Or, woman up.** Welcome to the real world. You are in charge now, you can mope around and wish for days gone by or you can make something happen.

2. **Make something happen.** I don't care what kind of job you have. Someone is watching or observing or depending on you. Know that redneck comedian, whatshisname, oh yeah, Larry the Cable Guy – even he knows what to do– "Git-R-done," he says. (Do I know popular culture or what?)

3. **Learn something new.** Unless you know everything already, chances are learning a new skill will help you break loose of the I WANNA PLAY all day syndrome.

4. **Don't wait to be told what to do.** You go find it. There is NOT a job around that is smaller than the person holding it. You can always make it better. Find out how, do some research, what do others in similar jobs do. It's like what my friend Eddie used to tell me at recess every day, 'tag, you're it,' he said.

5. **Some days you have more energy, right?** Right? What made you feel that way? Repeat.

JOBDIG RECOMMENDS: www.execareers.net

The Anti-Graduation Speech

(Admission: I once told a graduating class during a commencement speech that since they would not long remember what I said, the least I could do was to give them each a bag of M&M candy. That way, years later, if anyone should ask them about their commencement speaker, they could admit they forgot the advice, but say that they did get a free bag of M and M's, so all was not wasted.) Here is the speech I would give today:

Graduates, congratulations on finishing school. On other campuses, graduates are being told things like 'today is the first day of the rest of your life.' Or, 'It doesn't matter what you do in life, seek happiness and do great things, mostly for others.' 'Above all,' they are being told, 'Travel, see the world, examine how others live so that you may live a more full and complete life.' And, 'It matters not what you do for the next 10-15 years, who out there really knows what they want to do anyway, you will find your true passion in life if you look at each opportunity that comes your way.'

Hoo-ey. In case you haven't noticed, your mom and dad have been working two, sometimes three jobs, to keep you in school and in cell phones. Their last vacation was when they drove you to school and stayed at the Holiday Inn Express an extra night. Please don't disrespect them and go home and announce your plans to travel for a few years before you 'get a job.' That there's plenty of time to 'join the rat race like them.'

Here is what you should do. First, it is axiomatic, that winners zig when others zag. Opportunities follow those who do not take the paths taken by others. If others are traveling and not working, that is a for-sure sign that those who don't, will win big.

If you want to have a full, purposeful and productive life, get started now. While others are wondering what their passion is, you should go out now and discover it by actually working. I am not so sure you can 'think around' this issue of 'passion.' Often, you need to see it up close and gritty to see what you adore doing. Try some things by working, not by watching.

In the next 20 years or so, your parents are going to start needing YOUR help. What kind of help are you going to offer them? They did their part, worked hard, did without. Remember tag? You are it. It is a much more competitive world than ever. Get used to it. Get to work.

JOBDIG RECOMMENDS: www.suemorem.com

Five Resolutions
You Can and Must Keep

In December of each year, advice givers start writing about New Year's resolutions. Mine are achievable. Ready, Go:

1. **Show up to work on time.** Or, be early.

2. **Clean up your own stuff.** If you pack it in, pack it out too. Contrary to popular belief, your mother doesn't work here. Truth be known, she is GLAD someone else has to teach you this stuff.

3. **Stay positive no matter what.** So what if your job is hard? Boothefrickinhoo. It is no reason to get all mopey and down in the dumps. Part of your job, and no one tells you THIS, is to generate a positive environment amongst the people you see every day.

4. **If you are bored at work, get over it, it's you.** Only you can figure out ways to keep engaged at work. A tip that might work for you – keep doing the stuff you do daily, but keep your eye on how it all fits in to the bigger picture. Chances are some boss has forgotten to remind you about how critical your job is, or can be.

5. **Do something extra.** We moved our office this week. You should have seen our young staff – all of them did extra things, carried furniture, boxes, partitions and bookcases made of concrete. No one complained, they simply pitched in and did extra, even though they didn't 'sign' up for this duty.

Now, if they would only clean the microwave after their exploding lunches.

What To Do When
You Don't Know What to Do

First, relax. Few people know what they want to do, really. James Michener said, "Anything we do before turning 40 is just training."

If you are thoughtful, you will figure it all out. Don't rush it. Have some experiences, variety to your life. Along the way, someone or something will trigger

JOBDIG RECOMMENDS: www.careerdimensions-dfw.com

some passion in your life. It happened for me when I was about 32 or so – and it happened out of sheer luck and timing.

What is important is to be ready for these moments. Get experience. Be open to new things. Try something. Learn. Ask for more responsibilities. Find someone older you admire, and ask him/her out for coffee. Don't ask, "What should I do?" Instead just listen, tell your own stories, listen to theirs. Above all, listen.

Dear Kid,
On Being Dropped Off at College

Dear Kid— We just dropped you off at college. Your mom and I left a bit teary eyed just like we did when you went off to kindergarten. This time it's different. We know you will never really be home again. It is a big life transition. Heck, we may even turn your room into that home office we always wanted. Kidding. Here are some things we forgot to tell you before we let you go.

1. **You really aren't all that special.** Sure, to us you are. But as compared to others, you may well be right in the middle. How you do from now on out, will determine your "specialness." In other words, tag you're it. It is a big, cruel world sometimes but it almost always rewards the traditional good things: discipline, talent, skill, attitude, and work habits.

2. **The choices you make now will linger with you.** College is a time for experimentation, we get that. But how you make those choices will set you up forever, not so much for those actual choices but how you make your decisions. Are you with the peer group or are your own person? The practice you get now with this decision making process is more important than the actual choice.

3. **Carry your insurance card all the time.** I forgot to tell you that.

4. **Make a lot of friends.** More than that, resolve to learn something interesting and unique from all them. They all have stories to tell, let them tell you theirs and they will want to hear yours.

5. **In your cell phone, please make us your favorites, and list us by Mom, Dad, or Home.** That way, when you lose it, someone might return it.

6. **You will see you can get by with new types of behavior.** You can stay up too late, drink too much, not attend class, and more things that we don't want

JOBDIG RECOMMENDS: www.teenarose.com

to know about. I don't want to be a rain cloud here on your upcoming fun, just be careful.

7. **Don't call us all the time.** I promise to tell Mom the same.

8. **Learn to think, but get some facts too.** You already know how to think, what you need to assume is that you actually don't know everything.

9. **Your favorite comment, "That is your opinion," is sometimes misplaced, even stupid.** Think first before you say it.

10. **Divide the cost of tuition, fees, room and board by the number of hours you spend in class/studying.** Are you, er, we, getting a good value for the money?

11. **If you think about it, this is a great time to change some things.** If you think you have been too introverted, change. If you think you picked the wrong kind of friends before, change. College is a great time to make those and any wishes come true.

That's enough for now. As always, good luck. Love, Daddy

10 Lessons a Dad Should Teach His Daughter

1. You can do or be anything.

2. Always be aware of your surroundings.

3. Assume goodwill, but carry mace.

4. Don't chew gum.

5. Sometimes it simply isn't fair.

6. Never act less than you are.

7. Wide-outs, receivers, flankers, and ends are all the same...they go out and catch passes.

8. Understand that we get just the same thrill watching you play soccer, doing gymnastics or dance as we do watching a football game.

9. You will have to be t-h-i-s much smarter, wiser, nicer. See number 5.

10. No matter what, when, or where – trust your dad.

JOBDIG RECOMMENDS: www.lifeaftergraduation.com

What To Do When You Get Bad Career Advice From Your Parents

One thing us parents are never short of is advice. Got a new boyfriend? Well, let me tell you what I think about him!!??!! Picking a college? Here's what you should do. Buy or lease? Rent or own? My way is the only way to do it, kid.

Why do we give advice anyway? The short answer is that we can. Who else in our own lives listens (somewhat) to us when we expound on almost any subject? Plus, we can guilt you into listening to us.

We earned the right to give advice. We were there when you were born. You were wet, sloppy-looking, bloody and still, even with that scrunched up face, we loved you dearly, unconditionally from that instant on. We stayed up with you, rocked you until we fell asleep, got up at the crack of 0-dark-thirty with you, fed you, cleaned up your, er, messes, burped you and pretty much adored you. We watched your stupid soccer games when you were five, laced up hockey skates, bought you game jersey after game jersey and took all your friends to DQ after. Net, net – we earned the right to give you our stupid advice. We ache for those times. You will see.

Which is why we love to advise you about your career.

When I was 26, I told my own dad I was getting out of the Air Force. You would have thought I had told him I had decided to be a bank robber. He was devastated by my complete and utter stupidity. Didn't I realize how good a job I had? How secure it was? How well I had been doing? How the future was so bright for me? On and on; on and on; on and on.

He had grown up in THE Depression and job security was huge. Huge. For me, not so much.

His advice to me was really for him. He would never had changed careers because that was who he was. And he couldn't get past that – what was good for him would be good for me, he reasoned.

Back to you. Take your parents' advice to heart. They do know you better than you think. And, they truly have your best interests in mind. And, they might, might, be wiser about these things than you give them credit for. To

JOBDIG RECOMMENDS: www.career-magic.com

keep harmony in the house, try these these ten things:

1. **Break down and simplify their objections to your plan.** You be the adult in other words. Treat these objections as problems that you need to solve. Don't just yell at them.

2. **Take these objections and think about each one carefully.** For example, if you have to take a financial step backwards, can you continue to live in the manner to which you have been accustomed? How can you reduce your expenses?

3. **Tell them stories about your vision for your future and of people who are happy in this new area.** In other words, give them something positive to think about rather than all the bad things.

4. **Throw it back on them.** After all, they trained you to be an independent thinker. Mom and Dad, you taught me to be my own person...why be disappointed when I am?

5. **Let them know you will own the decision.** You will either make it go or will be responsible for fixing it.

6. **Tell them that theirs is the only advice you are really getting and listening to.** Us parents just want to be heard.

7. **Don't bring up past arguments or grudges.** "I wanted to play lacrosse in high school" and "You never let me," is not a winning argument today.

8. **Show some of your back up plan.** Wow them with your savings account balance. Show them the reference letters. Show them the research you have done about this new career.

9. **Make sure they realize you have been thinking about this for some time.** Face it, us parents can remember when we spent a week making your Pirate costume only to find out on Halloween night that you had to be Darth Vader instead. Don't remind us of that with some half-baked idea.

10. **Listen between the lines to our advice, some might be good.** But at the end of the day...it's your life.

You know what? No matter what you decide, you can still come home and throw your crap all over the house just like old times.

JOBDIG RECOMMENDS: www.coachcompass.com

A Fifth Grade Do-Over

Remember 5th grade? Might have been 6th, who can really remember?

Back then, kids were split into two groups—those who cared and those who didn't. Kids who cared were organized, had new pencils, and even new dividers in brand new notebooks. The kids who didn't care couldn't find homeroom, didn't get signed up for the right classes and had to borrow a pencil from their neighbor.

When the teacher yelled, "Listen up!" when the class got out of control, the kids who cared did, and those who didn't, didn't. Therein lies the story of their future.

Good jobs, promotions, and non-McDonald's jobs await those who 'listened up.' You know this is true.

The world is full of the too-cool or the overlooked or the under-motivated or the un-educated; Sadly, these perpetual victims learned every one of life's hardest lessons except the one that mattered the most.

If this is you, and assuming you would like a do-over, what can you do now? Or is it simply too late, just because back in 5th grade you chose the wrong path.

Coaching Little League is Great Management Training

Management is all about coaching and where better to learn than trying to teach a bunch of ten-year-olds how to play baseball. Here is why:

1. **You learn that incremental improvements happen slowly.**

2. **Yelling at them slows the actual learning process or skill development way down.**

3. **Individual coaching improves their skills more rapidly.**

JOBDIG RECOMMENDS: www.jtodonnell.com

4. Positive reinforcement leads to the repeated behavior you want.

5. Meetings in the dugout are not the same as hitting grounders.

6. Putting them in the right position for their skill brings more success.

7. Finding one great player elevates the entire team.

8. Be strongest up the middle.

9. Mom's can bring the cookies but they can't hit.

10. You never know when the coaching will pay off in a big way, with a game saving catch by the right fielder.

How To Be More Likeable: 10 Tips

To a large measure, your likeability will lead to success or failure. It often trumps skill levels in surveys of HR people who are asked to name the most important characteristic of job candidates and employees. Other than 'don't be an asshole' what can you do to increase your own likeability? Is it really possible to change? Or, do you believe your likeability has been set by some cosmic forces, and that if people don't like you as you are, so what? BTW, being rich or good looking is not on the list. Here are ten characteristics of likeable people.

Number 1: No left turns.

Years ago, someone wrote about his 90-year-old parents' Secret to a Long Life. He thought they would reveal the "secret" as eating right, exercise and wine with dinner. But their answer? No left turns.

When he asked "why left turns?" his parents said they read that more elderly people die from car accidents than heart attacks. Old people often turn in front of oncoming traffic and with deteriorating depth perception, accidents happen. So, they resolved to never make left turns again. They made three right turns to get them going the right way. Some days, they would lose count and have to make seven right turns. If they lost track again, they just went home, they said. After all, they reasoned, there wasn't that big of a rush to get there anyway.

Such a simple solution to a big problem: No Left Turns.

JOBDIG RECOMMENDS: www.blitzteamconsulting.com

Same thing with how to make yourself more likeable. There is one simple thing, that every likeable person has: A Positive Attitude. But we all have positive attitudes; especially during good times. It is easy to have a positive attitude then.

What's more differentiating and difficult is how to have a positive, optimistic attitude when things are not going so well. If you can conjure up a positive attitude when things are bad, people will be drawn to you.

Here are some tips for you to help you develop your own positive attitude.

First, develop the skill of self serving illusions. When suffering from negativity, think about something good that has happened to you recently in a similar situation. Chances are, you were able to solve it. Get good at drawing on these success stories in your mind. We all need to remember these little jolts of optimism and positive energy. The more you do it, the better you will get at it.

Next, realize you can control your thoughts. Most of the negative people you encounter choose to be that way. I have never seen a birth announcement that says Mary and Bill Jones had a beautiful, but negative baby daughter last night at 10:52 pm. We learn negativity, and it can be unlearned. Distract yourself from it, think about other things, and move on. Don't dwell on it. After all, 'stinkin thinkin' decreases your creativity (scientifically proven!) and hampers your ability to solve the issue. Like my friend Roger Larson used to say, "the more you stir it, the more it stinks."

Lastly, positive people know that most setbacks can be attributed to external causes which can be challenged, fixed or changed, not them. Negative people tend to think these are self afflicted, deserved, and permanent wounds. I understand that becoming positive is a life changing process for people…and it is not quite as easy as this. There are books and books about this subject.

But again,….no left turns. Some times the solutions are easier than you think.

Set a goal for yourself. A simple goal – try to be positive for 30 days. Think about it and act upon it. Nothing can be more worthwhile. Can you imagine how powerful this one little change might make in YOUR life?

"In everyone's life, at some time, our inner fire goes out. It is then burst into flame by an encounter with another human being. We should all be thankful for those people who rekindle the inner spirit."
– *Albert Schweitzer*

Number 2: Be engaged, passionate.

Every strength taken to excess is a weakness. Which is basically why some philosophers and parents counsel moderation. Don't get too high or too low, don't expect too much, and don't go overboard.

Let me explain that first sentence a bit better. I had a boss once who was very articulate. He was actually a college national debate champion. Speaking well was a definite strength, he could literally mesmerize an audience. My boss was no cult leader, but being so good at debate, he could literally win almost any argument inside the company. One time we were figuring out a clever way to announce an event to our 100 sales people across the country.

He said, "Here's what we do, let's get one hundred carrier pigeons, tie the note to their leg, and send them out to their homes. Can you just imagine the impact it will have to have a carrier pigeon delivering our meeting notice?" After looking around the room to see who would be the first one to throw cold water on this idea, I said, "I don't think carrier pigeons work that way, map reading is not one of their skills." But, he was such a good debater, he wanted to go on and convince me that indeed it would be possible. Strength to excess.

We do like people who are engaged in life, who have that sparkle in their eyes when they talk about what they do. The more passionate you are, the better. Just don't go all Jim Jones on us.

It is easy to find passion. You can have passion about your kids, your hobbies, your convictions. The more engaged you are, the more interesting you are, the more we want to be around you. If you are one of those who keep looking for that one job where you can have passion, you might be wasting your time. Every job deserves your passion. I believe that every job has something about it that should make you proud of it or the company, if you give it a chance. Sometimes it takes a willingness to commit to showing passion before you feel it.

Once at a family gathering, I asked a younger relative about his job. Talk about showing passion, he said, "Can I tell you why I have the most exciting job in the world?" What a great line!! And he believed it too. He worked in a feedlot, by the way. And literally shoveled manure all day. He loved what he did, and more to the point, he was unconcerned with my preconceived ideas about HIS job.

If you are like me, you want to be around people like that instead of the people who are always searching for that one, stimulating job that gives them passion. You give passion, you don't take it. Sure, you can go overboard with the passion stuff, but I will still like you better.

Number 3: Be of good humor.

This is so easy to do, but we often get all wrapped around the axle of professionalism. We lose sight of the fact that we all love to laugh. Those people who make us laugh are the ones we want to hang out with. I am amazed at how serious people can be inside a business. For goodness' sake, smile a little.

Someone recently told me that his work environment was different, it was "old school," very professional and extremely serious. So serious that people didn't greet each other in the hallway, even. I told him that chances were good that the people wanted it to be more interesting and fun, and that he should lead the way. Changing the culture takes one person at the lowest level to get it all started. Company CEO's don't change the culture even though they take credit for it, people do.

Here are a few baby boomer tips to practice improving your humor. Watch The *Office*, *Boston Legal*, and the *Daily Show*. And then talk about it the very next day with someone at work... Eg., "What was your favorite Denny Crane line?" My favorite: James Spader's character was describing the new hot girl and commenting on her beautiful neck. "Denny," he said, " you should see her neck." Slight pause for effect, he repeats for emphasis, "her neck." Then Denny Crain (William Shatner) says, "She has two necks?"

Generally speaking, most of us already have good humor. We laugh with our friends. Simply use it more, even look for ways to use it more. Tell a joke, however badly then laugh at yourself, if it is THAT bad.

The world is serious enough without all of us contributing even more. I choose to like people who are of good humor.

Number 4: Assume goodwill.

Years ago, I managed distribution centers for my company. There were twelve of these centers spread across the US, and my job, circa 1980, was to make sure they served our distributors with timely and positive service. Service had gotten so bad that it was all the distributors/dealers would talk about, not how much more they could sell, but how terrible our service was and, for those of you familiar with third party sales channels when your distributors are upset, angry, it gets ugly fast.

So, after asking for this job that no one else wanted. I got the job of fixing them. I had zero warehouse, inventory, or operational-type experience. Zilch. I was told the DC managers were so bad, so non-customer service oriented, that I should just start over. I had free rein to do so.

Instead, I called a meeting for all the DC managers at the home office. Most had never been to the home office before. They had not drunk the company kool-aid yet. They arrived thinking that the new guy (me) was about to fire them all. They were scared, defensive and angry.

Even though they were uniformly described as malcontents and sloppy representatives of the company, that chances were pretty good, I thought, that they had simply been ignored. In short, I believed they wanted to do better but someone had to show them how.

Once they understood that I was not going to fire them, that I assumed they wanted to fix this common, not-just-them problem, we all buckled down and fixed it within a few months. They even proudly wore the uniforms I strongly suggested they wear while working at the DC location. Of course it helped that everyone in top management stopped by our meetings IN THE SAME UNIFORM.

My takeaway lesson was we should always assume goodwill in other people instead of jumping on some out-of-control, negative, ain't-they-awful bandwagon.

This works in almost all situations. If you are thinking negative thoughts about someone's actions, let your first thought instead be to assume goodwill on their part.

Number 5: We all like compliments.

This is a dicey one because it is very easy to overdo handing out compliments, but people who feel comfortable complimenting others and, who give them sincerely, are more likeable. Honestly, I have noticed that even paying untrue compliments has a positive impact.

Many people are starved for compliments and many spend entire lives without hearing something positive or complimentary. Please look for a way to compliment a co-worker or a customer. It is really quite easy.

Obviously, you must do this carefully. Just because you call a pig a horse, doesn't make him one. But there are plenty of ways to compliment on something he just said, compliment on a recent completed project without saying how you would have improved it or even on his thinking process.

I believe people like being valued and a well placed compliment shows them that you value them. Other compliment-rich areas include: Anything about their kids, their thoughtfulness, their thinking process, their departments, teams, company, their skills, even their voice.

Number 6: Control your insecurities.

I know someone who is constantly saying things like, "Well, it's not what YOU are used to or "I know YOU would never buy this, but it is ok for me," stuff like that.

Maybe he means well, and perhaps is trying to show a bit of humility, but to me, it comes across as being incredibly insecure. Admittedly, we all have a bit of insecurity, it is only normal and natural. But communicating your own insecurity often is a turn off to a lot of people. Therefore, to make yourself more likeable just watch how you communicate yours.

We all do this, I understand. Thankfully, we have people who are close to us who understand these moody comments and can help assuage our insecurities. But co-workers might be different.

There is a huge difference between admitting a lack of ability or skill actually a positive, likeable trait as in, I don't understand the issue or what I must do to solve this problem, and I guess I am too dumb to understand this issue here. I hope you can hear the difference.

Number 7: The trick to listening.

Since grade school, we have been taught or told to listen better. Trouble is, this is where most advice ends. So, when we hear that listening skills are important in all relationships, we don't really do much differently other than get a new, intense look on our face.

Good listening is more than that.

Here are some more tips to better listening. Listen, acknowledge and add something of value. One can't simply listen with a vacant look in your eyes...you have to acknowledge what is being said. This is more than "uh-huh, uh-huh." Say something back that lets the person know you were actually listening and thinking. Not too hard, you say? Sure it is, because you will be more concerned about your part of the conversation, WHAT WILL I SAY NOW?, than actually listening. The more confident you get and the better you listen, you will find that you are worrying less about what you will say, and you will listen harder to what they

JOBDIG RECOMMENDS: www.you-can-learn-basic-employee-rights.com

are saying. After you acknowledge them, you will become a lot more likeable if you add something as long as it is relevant and on topic.

We have known people who apparently listen but have that "what-I-am-doing-here" vacant look in their eyes. By training yourself to listen, acknowledge, and then add value you will be a better listener than 90% of all adults.

By listening better, even if you don't get to say too much in a one-sided conversation, people will think you are quite smart for taking such an active interest in what they are saying.

Number 8: Flexibility.

This has nothing to do with doing the splits or some yoga move. Peace out.

People who are willing to do new things, consider others' viewpoints, or learn some new skill are generally more interesting and likeable. There are some people who won't try a new restaurant, new food or a new type of entertainment. We are all different, sure. I don't like opera music on the radio. But if someone invited me to attend a local opera, I would go. Ok, I might not. We all have likes and dislikes.

But the more you are willing to accept change and are viewed as flexible and adaptable, you will be more likeable obviously.

Number 9: Manners. Grooming. Language.

Some think that having good manners is outdated. Far from it. People with good manners are most definitely likeable. If nothing else, most of us like being around people who have 'em. Just remember what you learned in kindergarten, or what Mom ragged on you about all the time. Say please and thank you, write prompt thank you notes, stand up when a woman enters the room, take your ball cap off indoors, use the right utensil, say excuse me, open doors and let others go first. Better yet, buy a manners book and work hard on improving yours.

I have noticed that some people have poor grooming skills. You would think this is an adult type skill, but perhaps no one ever took the time to explain these facts. Wear clean clothes, shower or bathe daily, don't overdo the cologne, brush your teeth. Seriously, how hard is this? If you choose not to do anyone of these things watch how people avoid you.

Personally, I like people who have good language skills. It's not that I dislike people who have trouble with subjects and verbs, I just notice is all. But even more than using proper grammar, I find myself avoiding people who use toxic language, swearing excessively, showing a temper, complaining or whining. And, gossip. If you are a gossip, just be aware that people will eventually migrate away from you. If you talk about others, the reasoning goes, you will get around to gossiping about me.

Number 10: Humility is endearing.

Genuine humility is very appealing to others. The issue is how do you attain it without being false or fake. All of us have known someone who fakes humility "Oh no, I couldn't have hit all those home runs without my hitting coach and his advice" as a way of generating even more compliments for their achievements or actions. This fake humility is transparent and communicates more insecurity than humility.

How can you make yourself more humble? Here a few ideas: Stop comparing yourself to others, old classmates and/or co-workers. Who cares what they are doing, instead how are you doing on your own path? Next, acknowledge your own faults. Trust me, you are not perfect. There is always someone better, who has more skills than you. Next, defer to others. Sometimes other people have better ideas than you. Review your past, ask yourself how you got to where you think are. Was it as a result of your own natural born charisma? Or perhaps just luck?

"After crosses and losses, men grow humbler and wiser."
– *Benjamin Franklin*

Chapter 5:

If you want to start a company: 100 mini-lessons

If you want to start a company: 100 mini-lessons

Sometime during your adult years you will wonder about starting your own business or company. Everyone thinks about it so you will too. There are a lot of factors than go into this decision and things you should know. Some people can achieve success on sheer effort combined with a great business idea...even if they have little experience or knowledge about business. I have made a somewhat random list of attributes and characteristics that most entrepreneurs have or develop quickly when they start their own business. I have included some suggestions for you as you contemplate this big step ahead.

1. **Speed reading will save you.** These days one needs to be able to read reports, white papers, newspapers, magazines, business literature and even blogs. If you are a reader that still sub-vocalizes each word, you just won't be able to keep up. I think the will to read and the ability to read fast is paramount to your start up success.

2. **A must-read entrepreneur reading list for you.** No list can start without *Atlas Shrugged*, by Ayn Rand. Next to the *Bible*, this was the book that most business leaders of the last fifty years have said influenced them the most. Reading this book will add to the fire in your belly. Next, *Solution Selling*. Out the 2,328 books on selling, this book is by far the best. It breaks apart each step of the sales process so almost anyone can understand how to make more sales, the absolute KEY in any start up. The second best sales book? *Conceptual Selling*. The third book is *Emotional IQ* by Daniel Goldman. I think creating a startup environment is as much to do with the culture and getting people to do things than anything else. Goldman helps the reader understand how critical managing your emotions can be in this process.

3. **Get comfortable asking for advice and help.** Although there are plenty of people who have created successful businesses on their own, most need help. They bring the basic skills and passion, but learning from others is absolutely paramount. If you are someone who knows everything, good luck. Seriously, good luck. There are many, many friendly resources that are willing to help you get up and going. You just need to find them, and ask for their help and advice. These folks LOVE and WANT to help you.

4. **Present your startup idea to anyone who will listen.** And even to those who won't. Startups do not reward security and safety. If you are hesitant about exposing your idea to others, you won't be able to expose it to prospects, customers and investors. Don't expect constant support either. Most people will say something like, "Yeah, that sounds good. You should do it." What you are looking for are those few who ask good questions or who challenge your thinking process and research.

5. **Get really, really good at concisely stating your business idea.** A lot of entrepreneurs fail in this area. It is important because you will need to communicate this to prospects, investors and new employees. What I have kept in my mind constantly over the years, is one internal question as I have started expounding on some idea: What will he say to Hilda at home later about my idea? Or, as a great friend used to say over and over again, "If it is fuzzy in the pulpit, it is really fuzzy in the pews."

6. **Find a metaphor that works for your business idea.** It will just help you identify your business to others. Are you the FEDEX of dog products? The Amazon of doll clothes? The Heath brothers have written a very clever little book called *Make It Stick*, which helps develop this theme more completely.

7. **It is about leadership, not management.** If you have not led people yet in your career, even though it is not a prerequisite for success: but you should get this experience. Basically, it is all about getting people to line up behind your ideas, embracing your vision as if it were their own and getting people to do things. That might sound manipulative...getting people to do things for you. It is just the opposite of being manipulative, it is more about giving up things, than controlling them. I believe there is ONE consistent trait of good leaders, which I will discuss later in this list. You can learn from the masters. This is where your ability to read will make all the difference. What is OUT THERE, are books from historical leaders that tell you exactly how to be a better leader. One thing you can do now, is to become a leader. Whether at home with your kids, by coaching or by volunteering somewhere. I think some of our best coaches got started by coaching kids' teams, for example. Getting the kid whose idea of a baseball game is a pile of dirt and a stick know when to tag up on third base is true leadership. Or, to watch the best leadership movie ever, rent the old movie "Twelve O'Clock High."

8. **Love your prospects.** This is a different and more specific than the axiom of "Be Passionate." This was really brought home to me several years ago, when I attended a new company investor presentation. After the very professional presentation, the co-founder was asked in a small, friendly group of people, if he had always believed in this approach. (The company was in the self-help space.) He said, 'No, I don't believe in it, but it looks like a wide open market.' If you are approaching the business from a purely economic standpoint, you might be able to make it work. All I am saying is it makes it all more fun and believable if you love the prospects and customers. Warren Buffet owns Dairy Queen and I'd bet you a marshmallow Blizzard that Warren loves DQ ice cream. One thing he would not say is, "Americans should not eat ice cream."

9. **Know what you are good at.** Chances are you are very good at one thing. You will be successful if you can get yourself in position to use your one thing more often. It is not a problem if you are not good in every facet of your business. It is more important that you realize that others can do what you cannot.

10. **Build your team.** Everyone knows building a team is critical. Here are some little things you might not know. Hiring a big-company-experienced-only person because of their industry skill is very, very risky. It seems to me that every big-company person wants to be in a smaller company. Frankly, it is condescending. What they don't want is exposure to a one-deep work environment. Just make sure they have worked for another company AFTER IBM or General Mills. Next, try to meet the spouse. I am not a big proponent of going out to play bridge or socializing if you don't want to, but I do think it is critical to assess whether the spouse is going to be tough and supportive enough. Next, if they can describe how doing their job will impact the customer, that is also key. Further don't hire any assholes. I want loyalty to the 'cause' no matter what. These few sentences do not do this topic justice, but you get the idea.

11. **What pain are you fixing?** Every new business must fix something for someone. It might be an inefficiency or a lack of a necessary feature. In my first company, Scott Drill and I fixed only one problem and it wasn't even associated with the better product that we had developed. The problem we fixed, or the opportunity that we took advantage of, was that the dealer network was being ignored by the acknowledged monopolist, Kroy. These dealers were upset, worried about their futures and angry about Kroy's new distribution method which was in direct conflict with them. When we presented our product to this angry sales network and pledged our constant focus, it was exactly what they needed and wanted to hear. Our product was better, but if we had not solved this real problem for the dealers, they would not have supported us or sold our product. Every new company needs a pain to fix. Varitronics, now part of WH Brady, was built on this concept.

12. **Can you handle pressure?** One thing you can depend upon is the amount of pressure you will be under. Some might be self-imposed, most will be from external sources. Sales people will want something easier to sell, investors want faster progress, others want more or less of this and that, and constantly. How you handle these pressures will go a long way to determine your success. Someone told me a long time ago, that my only job was "to make the comfortable, uncomfortable, and the uncomfortable, comfortable." I think that pretty much sums up the new company leader's most critical assignment.

13. **Get good at motivating yourself.** During tough times, can you do it? It is easy to motivate yourself when all is well. much harder, when it is fourth down and time is running out. Be self aware enough to understand this ability or capability in yourself. Find something that seems to work constantly, a self-talking mechanism that allows you to keep on keeping on. I can remember someone coming into my office one day, and asking if "something was wrong," if we were in trouble?' When I answered no, and wondered why he had asked, he said, 'Well, we have noticed how serious you have been and

not smiling, so we assumed something was wrong." Even the appearance of a motivated leader is crucial. So, what specific tips can I give to help with this self motivation? I think there are many different techniques from reading quotes and motivational stories to keeping it all in perspective. You are different than me in this regard. I have a unique ability to be just dumb enough to think that "this too will pass," and act accordingly. Notice that I said ACT. You should develop your own triggers.

14. **Detail vs. general.** Successful entrepreneurs know how to move from one skill or attitude to the other. I have seen people who seemed to know every detail about their business to those who can't be bothered with the nits and gnats. If you think you have to know every detail to achieve success, you don't. If you think you can get by only by operating at the 40,000 foot level, you can't do that either. The trick, it seems to me, is an ability to wander back and forth, and to pick your spots. If you tend to be detail oriented to the extreme, be prepared to make every decision in this detailed area. I know someone who has to approve literally every transaction for pricing consistency. His team knows this and the unspoken message is that no one else can be trusted with knowing how important pricing can be in their business. He ends making every decision…his people have been trained to act this way. Alternatively, I know someone who is so removed from the day to day operations, that he doesn't even attend company events, like Christmas parties, whatever. Both are successful. Both know the traits they have and have built organizations that have adapted to this reality. What they are, is consistent. In my own case, I don't like meetings. I am pretty sure this is fairly well known about me. If, all of the sudden, I were to start calling meetings right and left, people would wonder what happened to me. Or worse…they would ask themselves the most dreaded thing that can be said of an entrepreneur: "I wonder what book he just read to make him change his behavior so much."

15. **Storytellers needed.** Ever since Eve told Adam the story about the apple and the serpent, we have paid attention to storytellers. We listen better and learn more when we hear stories. Develop this skill and win. There are certain duplicatable skills in great story telling. Learn them.

16. **Be an active good listener.** OK, so you are in charge; Soon you will begin to hear only those things that your people want you to hear. People are awfully smart about what the boss needs or wants to hear. Your job is to develop a bullshit meter, a sort of internal device that will keep you steady and assured. From time to time, it is alright to let others know that your BS detection ability is operating. If you don't, the BS just keeps getting deeper and deeper. I had a boss once who, when he felt the BS was flowing fast and furiously, would simply raise his arm and say, "Everyone, save your watches…it's getting deep in here." We all laughed but we knew that he knew.

17. **Don't get all big headed.** One of the character traits of most entrepreneurs

is a well-developed self-assuredness. Never let this cockiness develop into a situation where you begin to believe your own press releases. I have seen this happen all too often. It has happened to me. In my own case, I have noticed that when I have had a positive story written about one of my companies. I generally get too much of the credit and I change somehow. My head gets a little bigger, I am not quite as hungry. My solution now is not to be involved in such PR efforts. In my own case, there is a direct connection to my picture being in an article and my own big-headedness. Now, some people love this and have milked this attention to the betterment of their business. I understand that.

18. **Pioneers get the arrows in their back.** I think it is far better to be second with a differentiated product than having to educate and build a market. Sure, both are possible. An early business hero of mine, Mike Vance, told me (and 300 others) that you can create something special by thinking up a new idea OR by re-arranging old things in new ways. Steve Jobs didn't invent MP-3 players, he made old ones better. Here at JobDig, we are not the first free weekly newspaper, we are simply the best with our new ways of serving our customers and jobseekers. There is success in looking at old offerings and improving them.

19. **Is work fun for you?** Do you laugh a lot at work? Or, are you serious? After all, this is a serious, not a comical endeavor. Part of the unspoken reason to starting up your own company is NOT to be your own boss. Truth be known, it is really so you can have more fun. If you can't picture yourself having fun, don't bother.

20. **TIVO ability.** As well we all know, TIVO is that device, the first DVR television attachment, that allows us to record and fast forward through television programs. It helps us avoid commercials. You should have a similar ability to focus on the future...even to see what it might bring you. You will be required to help others TIVO their own work, so they can see how their work will eventually contribute to the overall success.

21. **Delayed gratification is necessary.** Stretch your arms out to your sides. One hand is pulling on a rope and the other hand is holding the bell. Some people need the bell to ring at the same time as the rope is being pulled. Others don't. Often, there is a significant time delay between pulling the rope and hearing the bell ring in a new company. This is true whether you are investing in sales training or a new product. It is surely true when you are thinking up your own exit from the business. Things take time.

22. **Sales in number one, two and three on the priority list.** You should plan on spending most of your time worrying and working on your sales efforts. Nothing else matters much. A sale happens when someone pays you for your service or product. Don't get too excited if the marketing focus group says everyone will buy one. Get excited when someone pays for it.

23. **To sell many, sell one.** To build your company, you have to sell multiples. You can't just sell one. Anyone can sell ONE. The trick is to sell a lot, right? Sure. But before you can sell many, you have to sell that one single customer so that he is excited and pleased to have your product or service. This is why when you talk to venture capital investors, they are obnoxiously insistent on waiting until someone buys something from your company. Everything else is classroom.

24. **Family support, are they with you completely?** Some family members love the idea of being associated with a successful entrepreneur. No one questions that. But some family members will not share your dedication and persistence, not to mention focus. The last thing you would need is someone back home who questions every move, every decision, every investment. This is not to say that your family members have to be all stupidly supportive. It is especially powerful if you get good advice, support and an unwavering belief in YOU.

25. **Do you know what scalable means?** This is a relatively new business topic for an old business process. What this means is that you should try to develop processes in the business that can be easily duplicated and replicated. It is one thing to sell your product to one person, quite another to figure out how this sale was made so that you can make the next sale more efficiently. Success often hinges on your ability to continue to do the correct things faster and better that result in some tangible success.

26. **Ready, aim, fire.** Back when Beowulf was a lad, he used his trusty old slingshot to attack his enemies, kill squirrels and impress the maidens. Chances are he didn't aim all that much. What he did was just let 'er fly. If the rock fell short, he adjusted so the next time he got closer, and closer the next time. Same thing in a new startup. The situation favors action over planning. It really should be ready-fire-adjust. One of my favorite cartoons is the one with the two buzzards sitting in the tree waiting for the man to die from thirst... "Patience, hell," says one to the other, "I want to eat something."

27. **Can you sell dog food to the dogs?** This is one of those things that most startup people know and do instinctively. They know, and so should you, that the first group you need to sell on your idea, are the people inside the company. Too often, we tend to forget that every employee needs to believe. You can never miss an opportunity to re-sell them.

28. **Your sales people don't work for you.** The sooner you realize that all good sales people work, truly, for the customers and not for you, you will understand more about sales people than 90% of all non-sales people.

29. **Sales trumps all.** Sales will mask a lot of internal problems. Or, said another way....sales mean you can live to fight another day, and buys you time to fix and solve internal problems...which are sure to come.

30. **Just stay in business.** Too many new companies flame out, just like the after-burner on some supersonic jet. The pilot kicks in the after-burner for an added jolt of power, but once it happens, that's it, no more power. If you can just continue your new business, first year to the second year, then to the third year...chances are great that you will make it. Do whatever it takes to make it to that third year. Don't flame out.

31. **People sign up for vision, fun and principle.** Getting people to work for your new company will be difficult. You have nothing to offer. You can't offer great benefits, a brag-at-the-parties company reputation, or even middle market salaries. What you can offer is something no other company can match – vision—meaning you are out to solve some big, hairy problem that your prospects are facing each and every day. You can offer fun; mostly because every day will be something new and interesting. Lastly, you must offer adherence to principles. Treat everyone fairly. Be transparent and be honest.

32. **Can you ignore little things?** I knew we were well on our way to a good culture at JobDig when one of our reps brought in his dog to work. He didn't ask.

33. **Is there an enemy?** I would much rather have a company to compete against, a competitive enemy, than not. It makes your life so much simpler—all you have to do is make yours better, faster, cheaper. Everyone knows when you have reached success. When we started Varitronics, our basic mission was to put Kroy out of business. In a few years, we forced them from their monopolist perch to near bankruptcy. In short, we won. We started to flounder after that mission was accomplished because we needed another one.

34. **Incremental improvements almost always wins.** Too often we think we must improve in a dramatic fashion. All it really takes is consistent, small, incremental improvements in your new, developing business. Try to do one thing better each day.

35. **Are you OK with being in charge?** At the end of the day, in your new developing company, you are it. It makes no difference how complete your team or even how good it is, or how well you are doing. You are in charge, everyone looks to you. You need to figure out THE key success factor in your business and get all consumed by it. In Varitronics, our key success factor early in the business was getting our dealer network signed up. I thought it was so important, that I hit the road for weeks at a time, meeting and telling our story to potential dealers. Your consuming focus might be to get financing. This top line focus is your responsibility.

36. **Be ready for luck.** Nothing irritates me than someone saying how lucky we have been in our new companies, implying pure happenstance. It really isn't about being lucky, but it does involve being receptive to those moments where the stars line up to your benefit. When the Twins played in the 87

World Series, we were fortunate enough to get a bunch of tickets for our employees. I had a big sign made up, congratulating the Twins from our company. I asked some of our warehouse guys to get to the game early to get this big sign-poster up along the right field foul pole. They did. The next day our phone rang off the hook because our dealers were thrilled our sign was on TV as the announcers went to a commercial break. I guess we were lucky.

37. **Dream globally, think locally.** Sure, it is way fun to think about serving customers in every state and foreign country. You should think about your business in regional or international terms. Just be aware that your best, earliest and most leveragable sales and customers will come from your hometown.

38. **Break your business down to a few key metrics.** Far too many business plans say something like…"By only achieving 5% market share, we will be dominant in our industry." Ok, maybe that is true. Figure out a replicable, repeatable sales formula. Quick simple example: Let's say you send your customers a direct mail letter selling your small item. For every 100 you mail out, your costs including postage will be approximately $1 each. If you assume a 2% response (you have to keep this very practical and honest), two people will buy. So, you have invested $100 to get two customers. How much is each customer worth to you? We use to have a program we called "mail ten, call ten." Every day, our reps would mail ten new prospects and then call ten that had been mailed. It always worked. Nowadays, modern company leaders have access to a dashboard that is updated daily or even hourly. Know your metrics.

39. **On average, your people are not average.** This is a simple fact. If you were to ask for a vote and ask your people if they think they are performing below average, average or above average, most would believe they are above average. Your job is to be able to honestly assess their performance and to positively bring them up to their own perceived level. But keep in mind, each person is unique, special and has very different skills, and talents. Use them wisely.

40. **Assume waste.** And a built-in bias in your people toward doing less work. This is not being cynical, just realistic. You should understand that all of us waste time at work. Even more, there are many of us who, because of upbringing or whatever, have a tendency to avoid work. You can pay a lot of people to not do the work. I think you have to be very upfront with your employees and let them know you expect them to work. If you are blessed with a natural style that allows you to do this without pissing them totally off…more power to you.

41. **Be friendly but not so much.** This is touchy advice and actually hard to pull off, especially with employees who are more skilled and older than you. I believe it is one thing to be nice, friendly even, and quite another to hang

with them, and drink beer all day on Saturday. Your call. Your perceived friendliness will be an issue with someone not in the group. You want to be over-the-top fair with everyone.

42. **Are customers always right?** No, they aren't. In fact, some are unreasonable and even not profitable for you as business. Realize this fast. I am not saying you want to mistreat customers, far from it. But if a bad customer is negatively impacting you, your top performers and the business in general…fire them.

43. **Get more than 50% of your people totally engaged in the business.** If you have less than 50 employees your goal should be to get 50% of them…that is all you need..to be passionate and engaged in the business. By this I mean, if over half of your people think about your business after they leave work and are always thinking up new approaches, new solutions, then you are winning and winning big. That is awesome because most companies have an engagement factor of closer to 20%.

44. **Suggestion boxes suck.** I know there are a lot of management gurus who recommend having suggestions boxes spread around a business, to generate improvement ideas. If you need a box to generate such response, some other communication process needs fixing. If you ask for suggestions, you have to react to each and every one. Odds are, some won't be do-able. Now you have a negative moment in your company. You have to tell the suggestor that no, we are not getting a trampoline for those who need an afternoon break. (An actual suggestion for me, once)

45. **Formal performance reviews are de-motivating.** One of your biggest challenges in a start up environment is keeping the motivation high. Remember what it is like–no prospect knows your company (yet), the pay isn't all that great, you are working your people hard—all requires the utmost in motivational ability on your part. I was in the Air Force and like all military and large organizations, the AF had a very well thought out and detailed performance review system. They had teams of people being trained on it, how to give effective performance reviews and so on. It was documented ten ways to Sunday. It still sucked and it was basically a fast way to un-motivate people. I know HR people will have all this justification for formal reviews. Maybe they are needed once you get several hundred people. Insist your managers discuss performance on a daily or weekly basis with their people. They have the right to know how they are doing. Why make them wait for some artificial performance review deadline.

46. **Find a lead dog.** It is absolutely imperative that you find and nurture a top performing sales person. If you don't have such a leader, high level goals are nearly hard to achieve. Always keep your eyes out for this sales leader. He will help you in many, many ways.

47. **Put people in positions where they can be successful.** Get to know the

individuals and allow for difference. Helping them find success is now your job, not their mom and dad's. You must figure out what position or tools they need to do the job you are demanding of them.

48. **Know the lyrics, but understand the tune.** Business schools are very good at giving you the background and knowledge to deal with many business issues. What they are not good at is helping you know what to do when someone has an issue with drugs or alcohol. What do you do? What is your responsibility? What about trust? How long do you stay with a key guy who is not performing? What is the tune here? Can you hear it?

49. **Never talk down, talk up.** Disrespect shows up in small, insignificant ways. Your people can smell disrespect like bad gouda. Listen harder and talk less. Use 'and' more than you use 'but.'

50. **Don't dominate meetings.** This is incredibly easy to do; after all, you probably know more about the topic than anyone else if only because you have been thinking on it 24-7. If you dominate discussions, just expect to be in this position time and time again. Your job is to build a business, NOT your own self worth.

51. **Learn how to brainstorm.** Every startup does plenty of brainstorming and you should be not only good at it yourself, but have an ability to make others good at it as well. We all have heard the usual brainstorming 'rules': 1. Don't allow criticism of ideas; 2. Quantity over quality; 3. Encourage wild, even dumb ideas; and 4. Hitchhike on others' ideas. Here are some more ideas that will help:

   A. Have fun, laugh a lot.
   B. Stay on topic.
   C. Realize that some people will not be comfortable speaking out.
   D. Acknowledge people's ideas verbally and by their name.
   E. Brainstorm alone, first.
   F. Do not dominate the session yourself, talk less.
   G. It's a real skill to facilitate a good brainstorming session, learn by practicing.
   H. Not all brainstorming sessions are called that, most just happen.
   I. Think about the five senses constantly and how they impact the topic.
   J. Be one of the first to present a really terrible, stupid idea, then laugh about it.
   K. Don't give rewards or bonuses for good ideas – it will stifle future sessions.

52. **Be accessible and approachable.** Things happen so fast in the startup, that you must simply be there. This means in your office and where people are working.

53. **Model the behavior you require.** If you demand certain things, do those things yourself, better to a higher degree. This means getting to work on time, and so forth. I thought this one was too obvious to include, but alas.... it is not.

54. **Try not to use your own personal sales as the model for your sales team.** It is ok to sell, sure. But if you want to build others up to sell, be aware that you will own your customers forever, no one will want to jump in and serve the boss's customers. Plus be aware that you bring different skills to the sales presentation than the rep can bring. You might be friendly with decision maker or owner, for example, a luxury your 25-year-old rep might not enjoy.

55. **Can you recognize the top five problems in most sales departments?** This is generalizing and your own organization may have different issues, but here are five that I have seen over and over again:

    A. Lack of energy and excitement. For something to be sold, someone had best be excited about it, and your people can control themselves. Get them excited about your company and product.

    B. Product training is not sales training. Today, most sales training is really product training. If they are great at describing your product's features and benefits, but are not closing deals, it is the training.

    C. Too much talking, not enough listening. Most good sales people are great listeners. Do your sales people have lists of open ended questions to use?

    D. Alignment issues. It is like going to the doctor with a sore throat and saying you have a sore throat and having him start writing a prescription, "because you are the tenth person today who has that symptom." You still want to be examined, right? Same thing with a prospect, just because your sales person has seen the situation before, and believes your solution is best....he still needs to develop the process with prospect.

    E. Ask for the order. By far the biggest one. Remember that there are four things that can happen: A sale (good), no sale (good), advance the sale (good), or continue the sale (bad).

56. **Focus on the big picture but don't allow ANY typos.** This is a very touchy area, because you should be able to see the business from a 40,000 foot level, but if you are always up there, small mistakes happen that will undermine your credibility and professionalism. For example, I am particularly picky on any materials in print about our company. My most common 'catch' is the comma or period and quotation marks. They go "here." Not "here".

57. **No matter your benefits budget, it is the gift-giving thought that counts.**

One time after a particularly good year, we announced a huge (for us) contribution into the company 401k plan, hundreds of thousands of dollars. Which got a polite response from the Christmas party crowd. But then, we gave each employee a watch with our logo on its face. People said it was the best gift they had ever gotten from a company. There are tons of books on this subject—Bob Nelson has made a career out of this topic alone. His book *1001 Ways to Reward Employees* is good, but you can think up ten of your own ideas as you drive in to work tomorrow.

58. **Talk to your competitors, don't run from them.** This may be a bit counterintuitive and it might not work well in your industry, granted. Talk to them at trade shows, conferences, even on the phone…don't talk strategy or tactics, talk about the industry in general. You can learn a lot by talking to someone who is confronting the same issues. One never knows what you might learn. Here at JobDig, we compete against a daily newspaper out in North Dakota, the Fargo Forum, in a very limited way. We both sell help wanted advertisements to employers in the Fargo area. The Fargo Forum owns a bunch of local newspapers and we had an idea of how we could partner with these local papers. Obviously, we knew we had to offer some unique benefits, we understand that. Anyway, I called up the publisher and after several attempts finally got him on the phone. Introduced myself. He told me they had no interest in meeting, even to hear our ideas. Keep in mind, JobDig has taken over a million dollars out of their pockets, easy…more actually. And I was calling, volunteering to meet. Here is the takeaway, if your competitor calls and wants to meet, for goodness' sake, meet…if nothing else, to size up your competitor.

59. **Communicate with your stakeholders often.** I don't care if your only stakeholders are family members, communicate with them frequently and regularly. If you have investor type stakeholders, this is a requirement. Far too often, we tend to forget our supporters. Let them know how you are doing, the good and the bad. They want to help you. There is nothing more fun than helping someone get started in a new business. By not communicating with them, you are robbing them of their biggest reason for supporting you and others like you. It does not have to be a big fancy shareholder letter, either. At JobDig, we write a monthly one-page, tongue-in-cheek, funny yet accurate newsletter that we send out to our stakeholders. We get constant good feedback.

60. **Join clubs….or not.** I know some advise new business owners to join the Chambers of Commerce and groups like Rotary and Lions. I know this works for a lot of people. I happen not to be a joiner…I know it would probably help me reach out, get to know more people, etc., but it is not ME. The point here is that you have to be true to yourself, no matter what the advice. If you cannot do it and feel good or comfortable doing it, don't. The world

is full of quiet, behind the scenes, unknown entrepreneurs building great businesses.

61. **Better to be OCD, than ADD.** We have all worked for, around or under bosses who had bad cases of ADD, Adult Deficit Disorder. They can be so random that many cannot follow their train of logic or directions. How about those Vikings? If you are to have a disorder, it would be best to have OCD, obsessive-compulsive disorder. In fact it may help you, word is. I have not yet met a successful entrepreneur that wasn't compulsive about something. Have you? Have you? I mean, really, have you? The worst boss, according to comedian Dennis Miller, is one who is both ADD and OCD. He moves from project to project, whatever gets his attention...but then he gets really focused on it, until the next project comes along.

62. **Shiny pennies.** Invariably this happens to the new startup guy. A new hire is made and then, all of the sudden, this new 'blood' captures your interest, imagination and focus. I have personally made this mistake more than once. It is a very easy trap to fall into, believing that a new person on your team has all the answers. Chances are he doesn't, and in the time it will take you to recognize this, you will have alienated your existing team. Be excited about new people but make them prove themselves. Dance with the one you brought to the party.

63. **People who say they can raise money for your startup usually can't.** I don't care how smart, connected or rich their friends, this almost always does not work. This is your job. Talk to them, yes, but never stop raising money your own self.

64. **When you are forming the business, do it the simplest way possible.** If you are raising money from outside investors, use common stock, not preferred. Use an attorney to get the paperwork done correctly. There are no shortcuts to this, a necessary, but saving requirement.

65. **Explore every possible sales channel.** One of your jobs is to understand how your industry takes products to the market. Basically, there are two methods–direct channels, meaning you sell directly to the customer; or indirect, meaning your customer is a dealer, distributor or agent who, in turn, sells your product to his customer. You can sell via both channels but it is more complicated and requires product differentiation, perhaps, and a keen awareness of pricing issues. When we started Insignia, we didn't know which channel would work for our new sign maker for retailers. We literally tried and tested several channels (dealers, independent reps, private label accounts) before deciding to focus on direct sales, over the telephone.

66. **If you feel inadequate in a certain discipline, hire it.** None of us can be good in every single area of a business. If you are not especially good at accounting, hire someone that is very solid and strong in that area. No one will fault you if you are not the best in that area, they will fault you if you try

to BS your way through these issues. Your job is all about building a team to execute a well defined plan. After raising startup money...that is it.

67. **Be wary of consultants, headhunters and every other outsider who wants to "advise" you.** I have paid for this lesson a LOT. At Insignia, I was seeking outside venture capital after investing a lot, for me, in the product development. I knew better, but when the potential new investor said they would only invest after their market research firm did a complete study, I said yes. The market research study cost us about $20,000 to complete and yes, you guessed it, they recommended that the venture firm pass on our opportunity. Like I had any choice at that point?...we HAD to make it work.

68. **Do not do any advertising or promotion that is image related.** Make your advertising pay its own way, with measurable results. It is not about image or some advertising awards, it is about generating leads that turn into sales.

69. **Test and roll, test and roll.** This is a slight variation on the ready-fire-adjust theme but an important one. Break down almost any offer or product launch to a smaller, focused and measurable size. If you want to be the best asphalt paving company in the metro area, try your new business in one small suburb before you undertake a metro-wide ad campaign. Test a few variables to make your offer the best possible.

70. **Never hire a quitter back.** Chances are, people will leave your company. No one is irreplaceable, it happens. But if they resign, do not hire them back into the company. It is a very, very tempting to do so. After all, you are a great person, and they made a mistake (they will tell you) in resigning, what have you. If you do, you have just signaled that your company has a safety net, and more people will leave to test the employment waters. Let it be known if they leave, that is ok, but they are not on the team now or in the future. The ONLY exception would be for Peace Corps volunteers or people who join the National Guard.

71. **Assume goodwill; but audit, measure and lock the doors.** I really believe in the inherent goodness of most people. This is true of your employees, customers and any other stakeholder you might have in your new business. In other words, don't go out looking for trouble where none exists. At the same time, realize that nothing gets improved until it gets measured. Only then can you understand if you got the result you needed...without concrete measurement devices, you are running a hobby business. Lastly, lock the doors. I loved my kids, but I still checked the liquor cabinet.

72. **It takes 4x the money and 4x the time.** Twenty years ago, they used to say twice the money and twice the time to get almost anything done in a new company. Now, for me at least, it is closer to four times both. And, that is starting with a start date and money amount that was developed with some experience. It is so easy to underestimate both. Build your plans around this four times rule, and you just might have enough of both left at the end.

73. **If your customers have to change their behavior, prepare for a struggle.** People are extremely resistant to changing their behavior. Can it be done? Sure. Keep asking yourself if there is a way to make their current behavior simpler, faster and cheaper—that is much, much better. I have a friend who started up a home delivery grocery business. The business invested tens of millions in systems, warehouse and customer acquisition strategies. Even though it is still operating, enticing the grocery shopper away from bricks and mortar to online has proven more expensive than planned. And, their value proposition is very compelling too. It is like the HR manager one of our reps talked to not long ago. "The daily newspaper just doesn't work for us at all, any more, " the HR manager said, "but we are still using them." When our rep asked why, she said, "well, my boss won't approve any other media."

74. **No one will like change, except you.** If you are starting to be successful in your new business, be prepared to cope with the newfound lack of flexibility in your team that will drive you nuts. You must always be on the lookout for new ways of doing things, of new products to add, and new customers. You might be the only one truly comfortable with ambiguity. Recognize this fact, and tolerate this resistance. Think of it not so much as a governor on your own creativity, but as voices of reason and carefulness. You are all about growth. Hey, mean well. Just don't let them start patting you on the head like old Uncle Curly who has Alzheimer's.

75. **No one cares as much about it as you do.** Your new company will consume you, and even most of your employees. Realize that most other people will not have heard about, or even care that you have a brand new widget. Your big dilemma about increasing prices?...they won't even recognize it or care. As one old curmudgeon told me once, "We are nothing but pimples on the ass of progress." I got the message.

76. **You can't stop certain activities, even sales, once inertia and momentum is working for you.** Every year at Varitronics, we would introduce a new product that we thought would kill our last one. Most of the time, it never did. People just kept selling and buying the older products. Once the train starts going down the track, it is hard to announce a big change, so don't expect immediate implementation. However, never ever announce a product before you are completely ready and it is deliverable. Sales people excel at selling products that they cannot deliver. It is much easier to sell blue sky than something tangible.

77. **Be gender, color, and politically blind.** More than a legal requirement, it will make your business better. I extend that to politics too. You simply cannot win taking one side or the other. To me, this means no political meetings, bumper stickers on cubicles and so forth. After all, I hate YOUR candidate, and all pretenses of goodwill and logic fly out the window. Don't subject your workforce to your political leanings,...or your customers, either.

78. **Have an under-promise, over-deliver mentality.** It is one thing to have the over-the-top positive attitude, which every stakeholder and employee will love, but quite another thing to make promises you cannot keep. Be positive. As Steve Jobs said, "Great companies ship."

79. **Handle bad news internally.** There is nothing worse than seeing a business leader relate bad general news to people inside his company. I am NOT saying be stupidly positive and not realistic. What I am saying is that if your market is experiencing some tough times, work extra hard at making your product line or service offer better. If you participate in any pity-party that might be going on in your company, you have lost. I don't care what the subject is, your job is to never-ever give up and never-ever admit a negative. Your people need to believe that no matter what the danger, you are going to lead them to the promised land.

80. **Worry is the misuse of your imagination.** Your job is to find another way around the barn…if this way is blocked, you need to find another way. It is not good enough to simply worry. Anyone can 'worry'–your job is take that negative emotion and solve the problem.

81. **No procrastination, in business matters.** A startup requires fast action and faster decisions. Larger companies can allow problems to evolve, even mature before someone takes action. Startups cannot. One simple way to determine if you are dealing with a startup mentality is: this person will not wait for a return phone call, he will simply keep calling and leaving messages. This may not be an endearing trait, but it is a consistent one of most entrepreneurs.

82. **An internal voice that keeps saying, "Why not do it this way?"** Or some variation of the same question. It does not matter if you are out eating or at a ball game, the startup person is always thinking of new ways of doing things. Tony Christianson of Cherry Tree Ventures used to have a drawer full of business ideas, actually concepts that needed 'starting.' Most of the time, the ideas come from impatience or unhappiness about a current product or service.

83. **Tested under fire and managed ok.** David Pomije of FuncoLand used to recommend that entrepreneurs go through bankruptcy at least once. You don't have to go out and avoid debts by declaring bankruptcy, there are other ways. I have a good friend who had his own investing company, and got several of his friends into a questionable investment. When it exploded, instead of avoiding his friends and rationalizing it away with a cavalier "they had the offering documents like I did," he knuckled down, and paid them all back out of his own pocket. If he called me today and said he needed a loan to start up a new business, I would send him some money, no questions asked. Also, the entrepreneurs who have been members of higher level sports teams have experienced tough times, of being behind, and have had

to perform at higher levels than they thought possible, they have been tested enough.

84. **Worry less about the big competitors and more about the guy in the garage.** The typical new entrepreneur is overly concerned about what General Motors will do about his new anti-litter device that attaches to the backseat. I actually experienced this almost exactly. A guy had developed a molded mini-trash can of sorts that would attach cleverly inside a Lexus. His question of me? How could he protect his idea from Toyota, the parent company of Lexus. Now I am sure this must happen, but I have not seen it. Most of the time, the large company will completely discount and disregard your offerings. When Scott and I started Varitronics, Kroy Inc. really discounted our offering, even made fun of us personally. This is more common than you would think—so don't worry about the big guys, worry more about the guy just like you, with a slightly bigger garage.

85. **Be thinking about barriers to entry, not products.** Every product can be designed better: Fact. Just because you have the best product today, does not mean you will have it tomorrow. Someone will make it look better, work faster or cost less. If you are in software, this might take just weeks. You can create a significant barrier to others who want to enter your niche or space, by thinking of every part of the business process as something that can be improved. In JobDig, for example, we can create our weekly newspapers, each unique with dozens and dozens of graphically perfect display ads, in a few hours. The problem we solved was how to scale the graphic design function without having dozens of graphic designers on the payroll waiting for Friday afternoon closings. This ability is a significant barrier.

86. **Get excited about little things.** A lot of the incremental improvements in a new company are fairly small and seemingly insignificant. The entrepreneur needs to be able to get satisfaction out of these daily little achievements. They intuitively know that little things done well add up to a successful bigger event, a launch of a new software release, for example.

87. **Can stay UP all day.** This is harder than it sounds. This is like performing on stage, with two shows daily. Your apparent self confidence and attitude will work wonders on associates, staff and stakeholders. They feed off this confidence and attitude to help you create the business.

88. **Sunshine pump.** Let's say you are having a bad day and a friend calls you. He is obviously down about something, almost depressed. One, can you hear it in his voice and two, by simply talking to him over the phone, can you make his day brighter?

89. **Business math in reverse.** Good startup people can walk through Costco, or a car dealership or listen to a highly paid business consultant and figure out the metrics, or the math behind the economics of the products or services being sold. They know what a direct sales effort costs, and even know

what the going rate is for a poor, mediocre or stellar sales rep. They know the margins required for indirect distribution and can calculate quickly what each level in the distribution chain must pay or cost. This back-of-the-envelope calculation is often the beginning stages of a new company, because it exposes an opportunity.

90. **A builder, not a maker, nor operator.** Creating a new business where none existed before is a unique skill. I don't care if you built it by being the best inventor or maker, or even if you happened to be the best manager of a certain function. If you built it, even if you started from another discipline…you built something new from scratch, from zero. Before you came along, there was nothing. You may have made it or operated it…but mostly you built it. I know a young woman who is building her own cookie company. She is literally the cookie maker and the operator of the tools, mixing machines and so forth, but she is building a business.

91. **Trust instincts, but drop bad ideas fast.** If I don't believe in my own ideas strongly, how will we actually find the RIGHT one? I don't care if I am a universe of one, I trust myself more than some un-engaged focus group. And so should you. And, I never guaranteed that I would have only good ideas anyway.

92. **Grounded in experiences, developed in practice.** Successful entrepreneurs have all sorts of experiences. Bill Gates came from a rich family and dropped out of Harvard. Michael Dell was a college student, Ray Kroc was a middle-age, malted machine salesman. The point is, everyone has some experiences that help get you prepared. I was in the Air Force, and when I knew I wanted to leave, I asked my friend Marge Setter what I needed to do in order to be better prepared. She suggested I find a direct sales company and join it. I did. I learned how to build a team of other business owners selling products. I learned how to sell others on joining my team as well as selling products. There is nothing quite like the experience of buying products, storing them in your garage and learning how to sell them. For those of you who have this experience of HAVING to sell 'stuff' by the end of the month in order to pay rent, you will know exactly how it feels to make payroll every two weeks. Same thing.

93. **Screw security.** If you are all about safety, benefits protection, fast cars and big cigars, you might not have the real, down-deep confidence it might take. Actually, I am not sure it is confidence or stupidity—what it is, is a belief that no matter what, at the end of the day, you can figure it out, and make it all happen.

94. **Understanding of the Law of Requisite Variety.** This is a law described by cybernetician Ross Ashby which perfectly describes the creative entrepreneur. Basically, the law says that in any system (company, department, meeting) all things being equal, the individual with the widest range of

responses (the most ideas) will control the system. To me this means that the gift or trick is in promoting plenty of ideas, fast and furiously. The process is quantity first, then quality. Lots of people can sift and sort ideas, criticizing and developing. Your job is to get the most ideas on the table, from you or others.

95. **High energy.** This may be a work ethic mentality or a caffeine-induced edginess. I cannot recall one entrepreneur who appears sluggish or lethargic. What's even more apparent is that they are NOT energy suckers, but energy creators.

96. **Quick studies.** This can be very irritating to others, but these people hear the first sentence and generally understand the paragraph. They quickly get concepts, and are moving immediately past the product feature discussion to how it will get sold and supported..and improved upon. They get bored easily.

97. **Don't blame others.** Remember when mom told you about pointing at others, that three fingers were actually pointing back at YOU? What this meant to me, was that if something went wrong in a department or company, chances are it was my fault, my error. Knowing this has made me less likely to blame others, my challenge has been to do what I can to eliminate my own mistakes. Firing people is especially difficult because we know it was not their fault, typically.

98. **Engaging personality.** Do people like you? Here is a test: tell someone about your life so far, where you grew up, went to school, and so forth. Does your personal story engage them? Are they laughing, nodding their head, actively listening? The point is–you can tell. If your story isn't engaging to them , you aren't. It is not the story, it is you. Learn to tell it better. This is the first thing you should learn how to do.

99. **Honesty**. They are honest to a fault, if that could possibly be true. They tell bad news often and believably, but to the right audience. They are honest with themselves and certainly others. They will often not tolerate dishonesty in any form. Don't lie to them.

100. **Humorous.** I saved the best and most critical for last. Startups are full of pressure, and the release mechanism is humor. These people are quick-witted, sometimes profane, and love to laugh with people. They will say the most inappropriate things and at the exact wrong moment. People are not sure if they are crazy like a fox or simply crazy.

Chapter 6:

Best and worst career advice from other Dads

My dad told me to get a good job, with benefits that I could stay at for 30 or more years. I decided to drop out of college and sell vacuum cleaners door to door. After generating over $5M in revenue, I sold the businesses and now travel the world as a speaker and author.

- Dave Sheffield, www.theshef.com

"**You work for pay, not to play.**" – As an artist, this has been invaluable. People think that artists somehow live on thin air and should donate their work to any and every cause. One reason I have been a successful artist is that I conduct my art career as a business.

"**If you are good at what you do, you make it look simple.**" – After a lifetime of drawing, painting and sculpting, I make it look easy. It did not happen over night.

"**Make money when you can, there will be enough times when you can't.**" – As I have lived through economic ups and downs that this makes more and more sense.

"**Always do your best. Whoever is hiring you may not know the difference, but you will.**" – Pays off in the long run.

"**If you do not like your job, do something else.**" – I have been lucky to love my career as an artist. I cannot imagine having to bitch and moan about hating my job my entire life.

"**A crappy education and no skills equals a crappy job which equals a crappy life.**" – One must learn and develop constantly to succeed.

- Internationally recognized artist Pablo Solomon, www.pablosolomon.com

My father on MBA's: "An MBA teaches you to be CEO of GM. They already have one." She continues, "While I got an MBA anyway, I later saw his point: an MBA taught me enough about some subjects to be dangerous (or annoying to those who are truly skilled in those topics). But there were other topics I delved into more in the program – and those were most worthwhile. Still, now when younger people come to me for advice about grad school, in most cases I advise them to consider more targeted degrees.

Her father on growing a business: "if you want to grow your business, hire the best damn salesperson in the field. Since you won't be able to match their salary, offer them a partial ownership. Not some future promise. Give them ownership now." Kathryn admits that "I never was brave enough to take his advice, but maybe someday I will be."

- Kathryn Korostoff

From waitressing through college and way after college, trying my hand at being a realtor, a pastry chef, a wine buyer, an event planner, catering manager, back to waitressing then finally an office manager at an ad agency that led me to my own Branding & Marketing firm – with each new job that seemed to be going no where, my Dad always stood by and said "It will all come together for you honey. You are a problem solver, and that skill will make you very successful, this is all a part of the journey that will lead you to a successful career." And there have never been truer words, for every job I had contributes to my success today.

- Heidi Koontz O'Leska, Chief Intuitive Officer, www.intuitivefare.com

My Dad gave me two important pieces of advice.

1. **An education is something no one can ever take away from you.**

2. **Whatever job you take or do, make sure it's something you really will enjoy.** A person spends too much of their life working, if you hate your job it makes for a miserable life.

- Melissa Gasnick Cloeter, President, WINC, www.link2winc.com

The best advice my dad gave me about my career was to find something that provided me with meaning and money. He said that having a job that provided only money would lead to a sad existence because money alone does not provide happiness, but also having a career that only provides meaning but can't pay the bills will leave you miserable as well because you'll spend all your time worrying about making ends meet, but having the combination of a career that is truly fulfilling -and financially sustainable- is the way to truly have success in your career.

- Suzanne Skinner

EVERY time I ask my Dad what he thinks about my next career move, he ALWAYS tells me that it's not a good idea and then gives me a list of all the things that could go wrong. I'm 44, have had more than 10 major career decisions ... this has been going on for a long time!

After each conversation, I carefully considered what he had to say, considered what I really want to do, and then moved forward with my original plan. EVERY time, six months later, Dad tells me what a great decision I made.

Now I take his negative response as a sign that my decision is the right one! It's a little backwards, but it works!

- Sarah Shah, Image Coach, TV Beauty Expert and Speaker, www.sarahshah.com

Best advice: Do what you love and find a way to make money from it.....
That was my inspiration and I did it!!

- Karen Auster, President, www.austerevents.com

The best advice my Dad – a self-made entrepreneur retired from the grocery retail business – has ever given me is that when you're in doubt about a serious decision or situations seem uncertain, "buy time." Now I'm a self-made entrepreneur following my dreams and watching my adult children pursuing theirs. My advice to them is the same. And it's always served me well.

- Sue Markgraf, www.greenmarkpr.com

The best advice my Dad gave me was to "Love what you do, for you will be doing it every day." This from a widower who raised us and was a microbiologist for more than 45 years with over 47 patents for E.R. Squibb & Sons – now Bristol-Meyer Squibb. He has since retired and is now in the stages of dementia – so every memory is precious at this time.

On the flip side, the worst advice he gave me when I said I wanted to be a Drama or English major was to "become a teacher, settle down and get married and raise your kids."

Out of respect and I guess defiance, I combined the two – I took my love for writing and art and created a career and successful company. I also got married and have enjoyed raising two vivacious boys.

- Pamela J. Principe-Golgolab, Owner of PNA Associates Inc., www.simplyparenting.com

"You're never too proud to work at McDonald's." When my siblings and I were searching for summer jobs, an absolute requirement in our home, my dad wouldn't take "no one's hiring" as an excuse. When we'd complain about the level of work we were doing – which we often complained was beneath us – my dad would use his patented response to teach us the value of whatever work we were doing.

My dad has owned his own thriving construction company in Texas for nearly 15 years and he's never asked someone to do something he wouldn't – and hasn't – done himself. He stresses integrity and work ethic above all else and believes our greatest contribution is how we treat those less fortunate than ourselves.

- Erin Myers, Consumer Brands, www.ede/man.com

CH 6: BEST AND WORST CAREER ADVICE FROM OTHER DADS

In our large family, my Dad was a tall figure inspiring awe. He worked 6.5 days a week so when we saw him we worshipped him. AND we made sure he never knew when we screwed up (if we could help it, which was not always).

He and my mom communicated to us often that we were "not like the other kids" when we asked to buy what they bought and go where they went. It was not communicated as a put down but a lift up: we understood that they thought we were special, approaching perfect. (Side note: we knew we weren't and suspected mom knew too, but we sure wanted to keep that disappointing news from Dad.)

One day, as a young adult, I was running a consulting office in a college. I had snagged an envy-earning client, the Federal Reserve in our city, and was preparing to do a half-day session for them on a Saturday morning. The time had been set so as to end at 11 AM so that their Saturday could still afford a good part of free time. Letters had been smartly sent out to each participant outlining the session and enlisting their commitment.

All at once I began getting wind of much grumbling. I talked to the supervisor and she said nervously that they resented giving up that time Saturday NIGHT. I was devastated. When I looked at the letter I had sent out (it was a mandatory session so they knew they had to attend), the time I informed them of was 7-11 PM rather than AM. I wanted to crawl under the desk and just die! The session was the next day. It was cancel or face their wrath. We cancelled.

As luck would have it, my Dad called for something. I was mortified and certainly wasn't going to let him know I was not only not perfect, I was stupidly careless! He sensed I was upset about something and asked. When I told him what I had done, I waited for his cry of horror. It didn't come.

The response he did make, I'll never forget. He nonchalantly told me his remedy when he does things like this. (He does things like this??) He said very matter-of-factly, "I just figure out a way to make sure things are 100 times better after the mistake than they ever could have been before, so that the client is glad the mistake happened." Then he went on to recount, proudly, several ever more serious botch-ups than mine and how he handled them.

I was awestruck once more but for a new reason. Here was this man that even as an adult I thought to be perfect, from whom I did my best to hide the fact that I wasn't perfect, and he was telling me his usual response when he does something that is anything but perfect. I've never forgotten that advice, and I've adhered to it often (though probably not as often as I could have) given the number of times I've had occasion to.

- K.T. Conner, PhD, Center for Applied AxioMetrics, www.thinkingpattern.com

When I was a little girl, my father would often say to me, "Bets – (he called me Bets) – Bets – Nothing Sells Like Sex."

I always thought that was a pretty weird thing to say to a little girl. But that's my dad – crazy, creative, and often inappropriate. He was a freelance writer. I followed him into the trade, with a stint in advertising where his early advice came in handy. Hope you find this helpful, or at least get a chuckle from it.

- Sarah White, www.whitesarah.com

My dad was a union ironworker turned welding instructor and would always tell me "There are only so many hours to work in a day, you might as well make as much per hour as you possibly can."

This advice has served me well over the years and has always pushed me to value and quantify my contributions whether during a salary review with an employer or now as a small business owner negotiating contracts.

- Lori Wilson, Co-founder of Funnel Incorporated, www.funnelinc.com

My father Scott is an auditor for a major oil and gas production company. I have worked my way up, at 28, to a regional management role with the nation's largest privately held staffing and human resource consulting company. I also released a book on leadership for young professionals. I owe great advice from my dad for much of that success.

I often call my dad to discuss the latest in my career, challenges I face etc. After a particularly tough situation dealing with a couple of employees who were pushing the envelope and testing my boundaries, my dad gave me the best career advice I have received from him.

"David", he said, "be cruel, but fair."

I love it! Be even handed with everyone, but demonstrate a clear line and hold it no matter what. With bad paying customers, "cruel, but fair". With the troublesome employee, "cruel, but fair". Strong consequences given with an even hand, is better than a vacillating position where no one knows where you are coming from. Consistency with consequence builds a culture of high expectations and top performers. I've built a successful business as a result.

Feel free to use it, if you like it. He may have said it a little tongue in cheek, but I've built a $15 million business, worked on Capitol Hill in D.C., and published a book. And I'm not yet 30. What's the best advice? "Be cruel, but fair."

- David Lewis, SPHR, Express Employment Professionals, www.theemergingleader.com

My Dad, born in 1918, Samuel Taylor Hirzel Sr. gave me some great advice by being a wonderful role model. He was a natural networker, before that was even a word. Everywhere we went, someone came over to say hello to him or he went over to pay his respects.

Once when visiting London, someone came up to say hello in the hotel lobby. He was open-hearted, and had friends of every race and religion …again long before that became popular. I have tried to follow his lead and it has served me well and made my personal and business life richer and fuller.

- Cheryl P. Heiks, www.bewell.com

"Don't be a teacher," he told her, "they don't get paid much." According to Lesley now, years later, "Now that is true. But I'm in my 50s and I have regretted not being a teacher. I think I would have made a great one. So I teach people in other venues, such as being a scout leader when my kids were growing up, or teaching classes in adult education, etc."

Lesley owns her own business now, Pillowcasegram, and said her dad gave her the best advice on that topic, "Your worst customers if you own a business are your family and friends. They will expect discounts. Don't give it to them." He was right, says Lesley, they do expect discounts. But I tell them that my wholesalers don't give me discounts on the items I sell family and friends, so I don't give them a discount. Most understand. Some think I'm a "cheapskate," but they don't pay my bills, so I don't let it bother me.

- Lesley Rackowski, www.pillowcasegram.com

My sister and I were just talking about this the other day. Our dad was a hard-working warehouse worker for 30 years in the oil business. He told my sister recently that every time he got an increase in pay, or a bonus of any type, he would always contact his supervisor, and the company's top executive to thank them personally.

My sister is a doctor with a big healthcare HMO, and she said last week she got a raise, and Dad's advice was with her all day, so she decided to contact her executives and thank them. She told them it was always Dad's policy to thank those in charge, and let them know how much it was appreciated to have any increase in pay. She got back the most heartfelt email from someone at the top saying how nice it was to hear the appreciation, and that in all his years being in charge, she was the first person to ever thank him. She told me she felt good carrying out a "habit" that Dad thought was important. Here we are both in our 40's, and just when we thought we couldn't learn anything new from our parents, we did.

- Jennifer Bourgoyne, Founder of Czela Bellies CesareanWear, www.czelablue.com

The best advice I ever received in business was from my father. One day I asked him what something was worth and he said "Something is only worth what someone will pay for it." He went on to explain that you can have land that is valued at $100,000, but if someone is only willing to give you $10 for it, well that is what it is worth. In this economy that really hits home.

- Sasha Windes, www.freshandgreen.com

My father told me to find a career to fall back on so that I can help my husband if needed after all the husband supports the family and I won't have to work all my life.. oops.. that didn't happen. While I started off in education I have had several different careers and after I got divorced started my own business; that was 13 years ago. My father also told me that women are the supportive role to enable the men to run the companies. Talk about old school.

- Harriet Cohen, Training Solutions

My Dad spent 43 years working – 2 with his first job and 41 years at his second – that was the norm for his generation – his career advice to me was "get a job in a bank, it's a job for life" – now look at the financial industry. That was probably his 'worst' career advice, I took it – got offers from four major banks, took one of them and became a human cash dispenser after 3 months and hated almost every minute of it.

His best advice was "there's no such thing as a free lunch" – very early on in my career I was boasting about the fact that I had enjoyed a lunch paid for by a customer I was dealing with in a sales role – that's when his advice came out. He was right and still is, no-one ever buys lunch at business just because they want to – there is always an agenda – hidden or not.

- Paul Copcutt, Certified Personal Brand Strategist, www.squarepegsolution.com

When I was in high school in the early 80s, a time during which the economy was rocky, my father asked me if I wanted to go to college. I thought he was asking because he was having financial concerns...I answered yes, I wanted to go to UT still and asked if he thought there was a problem. He said there wasn't a problem at all but that he wanted to be sure I was doing what I wanted to do and not what he and my mother had hoped for me. (My parents both went to college, which is where they met.) Dad said that it was really important that whatever I chose to do in life that I should do it because I enjoy it and not concern myself with what others think...and he said to not select a career just for the money because I might someday be better off financially but miserable in that career. I took Dad's advice to heart, which is why I majored in journalism.

- Scott Tims, www.thepointgroup.com

I was next to the youngest of five children, so I heard "it" with all three of my older siblings, "Get a job with good benefits." By the time I hit the workforce I knew what to look for – or so I thought.

My parents were both raised in rural western PA (near Pittsburgh), and my Dad worked various blue-collar jobs as a welder, pipe fitter, mechanic, etc. I thought we had a good life on our eight acre hobby farm. We attended a private school, had horses, cows, and a huge garden. But in my Dad's day, the better jobs had "benefits."

Fast forward to 1985 when, as a newly-wed, I found work in the Dallas-Fort Worth area in one of the "benefit-drenched" savings and loans. We had awesome medical benefits, PCS cards (any prescription was $2.00), three weeks paid vacation after five years of service (more for those who stayed longer), killer discount interest rates on loans, free snacks, free soft drinks/juices, ridiculously lavish after-hours parties (complete with alcohol), "semi-monthly Happy hours," and if that wasn't enough – they would pay you to go back to college and earn a degree (or get another degree), they would match a portion of your IRA/401K contributions...oh yeah, and they reimbursed you for your day-care costs if you had children in a day-care! Did I mention season passes to theme parks?

What about me? I was never sick. I never went to the doctor. I didn't party or drink. I hated school when I was in it, so I sure wasn't about to spend every evening (being a newly-wed man) back in a classroom, I only went to one or two of the company parties, for the first five years of my marriage we didn't have children – although later on I took advantage of the day care reimbursement for a few months. I never opened an IRA/401K. I hated theme parks. I DID drink orange juice or a pop a few times a week, and I loved the free Orville Redenbacher pop corn. I wanted a career with horses, but...you guessed it, no "benefits."

Today I live in rural southern Ohio and pastor a small country church. The people treat me very well and even pay for my continuing education (I make myself take one class every other semester). I love my work and I love my congregation. My family is rarely sick, no one has ever had a broken bone, been hospitalized or has ever been on medication. I still have no retirement plan. We are still happily married (almost 24 years). I have 6 horses, my office is in my home, we eat good, exercise, homeschool, and if I never received another "benefit" in my life, I would be happy and content. My life has been rewarding, but if I had to do it over again, I would not have adopted my father's perception of "benefits." Instead, I would have followed my heart and become a professional horseman; enjoying the "benefits" of waking up every morning anxious to do something I love. Today, I counsel my own children to follow their hearts and to "make it work." Life's too short.

- **Timothy Palla, Pastor in McDermott**

My father, Roland West, advised that if you can manage it, live to the East of where you work. It makes it so that the sun is not in your eyes when driving to and from. I've had that situation and it is nice. Right now, I walk to work.

- Carl West, Co-owner of Prospect Hill Forge: The Blacksmithing Classroom, www.prospecthillforge.com

When I was 20 years old, I dropped out of my first year of university where I was studying archaeology, realizing it was not my passion to shift shards forever. I wanted to transfer to a different college, one with a reputation for good, "practical" degrees - such as the Early Childhood Education program I was eying. As it happened, that college also has a respected journalism undergraduate program and my father, a 25-year journalist at the time, suggested I attend that program instead. Certainly my marks were good enough - I had earned a full scholarship to the first university I attended (and gave up after less than 1 year!). I resisted, and told him I loved children and would be satisfied in a career working with them. That's when Dad pulled out the big guns: he told me that, at best, a day-care worker might make $20,000 a year, while a journalist would easily make upwards of $50,000.

I applied for the journalism program next day - the deadline day - and was accepted. Since graduating in 1987, I have worked as an editor and writer at daily newspapers, national magazines, and now am a web editor and writer at my own business, writingSEO.com. I couldn't be happier with my career - and I owe it all to Dad's advice. (I still love kids; I just chose to have my own instead!)

- Heather Angus-Lee, www.writingseo.com

My father is one of my best mentors, still today. My father would always give me little tidbits of advice, but the way he did so was in a manner that left the choice and responsibility on me so I never felt like he was "telling me what to do." (Pretty important during my teen years!) When I took my first job he explained that people are hired for jobs because the employer needs something. The boss will be looking at who does a good job, who can he/she depend on, who is on time, and who is loyal. The boss uses this information to decide if it's worth it to keep an employee and they will look at things like this when deciding on who is getting promoted.

When I took a job as a waitress, he told me: 'If you pay attention to the coffee drinkers and never let their cup get less than 1/2 full, you will get better tips." He was correct! Had he told me "Don't ever let a coffee cup get less than 1/2 full." I probably would have rolled my eyes and went on. Instead I made a lot more money than my colleagues!

Another time I was chastised by a boss for joking around with a coworker too much. We were laughing and having too much fun for the environment, and not paying as much attention to customers as we should. I had always been a conscientious employee but when my friend came to work there, I started getting into trouble. Rather than get on my case, he continued to read his paper and said "You will always be making choices in your life as to whether you will lead or whether you will follow." A little later he pointed out, "Your coworkers are either going to be giving you a hand up, or grabbing your hand and dragging you down. It's up to you to make the decisions about who you surround yourself with." Rather than telling me what to do, he would just make observations and leave the decisions on my shoulders.

One of the most valuable lessons my father taught me was how to make a decision. I would ask him for advice and he always refrained from giving me a direct answer. Instead, he would ask me questions. What are your options? What are the negative and positives of each of those options? Does this move you closer to your goals? If not, are there good reasons or benefits that would be worth postponing the goals?... Then when all the information was on the table, he would tell me he had faith that I would make a good decision. He also helped me understand that it wasn't always clear what decision to make and that it was ok to make a decision and then realize it was the wrong direction.

Essentially he taught me fail forward. The message I internalized was "Do the best you can and keep getting back up and trying again." This served me very well in having the confidence to take risks through life. One of the most comforting things my father often told me at the end of conversations involving difficult decisions was "No matter what you decide, no matter how it turns out, you will always be my daughter and I will always love you." I didn't always make decisions that made my father proud, yet he was always true to his word. He loved me through the good times and loved me through the bad.

When I was about eight years old he taught me not to blindly follow authority. My dad preached at a little country church on Sundays. On Sunday nights and Wednesday nights we would visit other churches of many different denominations., I became confused wondering what religion we were. He told me we were Christian. Well if we were Christian, then why did we go to other churches that believed different doctrine. His words live in me still today. "You can learn something from everyone. Listen to whatever they say, then see what resonates with you. Take what does and leave the rest." This taught me to never blindly follow any man. It also taught me discernment.

Today I am an international keynote speaker and trainer and people often comment that I seem to be a very wise woman. Thanks to my Dad, Norman Rogers, I think they are right!

- Dr. Dee Yoh, Founder of Pablo Art Refinery and Gallery, www.deeyoh.com

My father told me I would never amount to anything when I grew up. I used that "career advice" as a catalyst and motivation to succeed.

- Gary Parkes

Both the best and the worst career/job advice that my dad gave me came in the same sentence: "Work for me." I did. I will say that through careful management of the relationship there has been way more positive than negative. And now I'm one happy S.O.B. ...that's 'Son Of the Boss.'

- Jamie Wells of Jamex, Inc,

My dad told me, "Be careful how you treat people on the way up the career ladder, because you might meet the same people on the way down." This has held me in good stead over 40 years – no matter how I would have loved to tell off colleagues and superiors, I kept my council. And indeed, as an editor, writer, and publisher, I have given (to my benefit) and received opportunities I would have missed if I burned my bridges behind me. Of course, I've given the same advice to my kids.

- Jesse Leaf

About 8 years ago I was totally down in my job. My bosses were tyrants and you never knew whether you were going to get Dr. Jekkyl or Mrs. Hyde. I complained a lot about the situation, but would never do anything because there was this insecure part of me that thought all of the horrible things they were saying about me were true. I was stuck.

One weekend I flew home for a wedding that I attended with my parents. At the end of the evening my father took me into the cigar bar at the venue and we ordered a drink. He looked me right in the eye and said, I am sick of hearing you complain. I want you to come up with a business plan and present it to me. If I think you have a viable idea I will fund and support you for one year so you can get your feet off of the ground.

That evening was a major turning point for me. My father had started his own business about 20 years ago and has been very successful. I respected him and wanted to follow in his entrepreneurial footsteps. So I pulled my resources together and now seven years later I run a successful marketing/pr firm. My business partner and I work with clients in the publishing, tech and healthcare space, we have invested our money and own real estate. Our goal is to retire in about 8 years and move on to something else.

Without a kick in the pants from my father I would not be where I am today.

- Michael Volpatt, Larkin/Volpatt Communications, www.larkinvolpatt.com

My Father said simply:

Best: Make sure you always think you are the smartest guy in the room (even though you may not be)

Worst: Follow the money, not your passion.

- Shaun Dakin, CEO and Founder, www.stoppoliticalcalls.org

Best and worst advice my dad ever gave me? I'm still trying to figure that one out, as it may have been both at the same time!

My father was in the oil business back in the 70's & 80's, and had a best friend that was a corporate pilot. They took me up for my first flight and, though I was initially terrified, I was hooked on aviation ever since. The stories they exchanged, as his friend lost jobs from airliners, or through different mergers led my father to discourage me from taking an aviation career. The one line I'll always remember is "You're really just a bus driver, baggage carrier without even the job security they have."

Well, it could be true, and I still dabble with flying, but have never pursued it as a career. I alternate from kicking myself for not going for it, to being thankful when I watch what continually goes on in the airline industry.

- Darrin Guilbeau, President of Silicon Advantage

Three years ago I published a book called "*HARD SELL: The Evolution of A Viagra Salesman.*" I took a circuitous route in fulfilling my dream of becoming an author. My dad unknowingly started me down the path with the advice he gave me when I decided to get out of the Army in 1995.

First, he told me I was "an idiot" for leaving the Army, as opposed to staying in 17 more years and getting a full retirement.

Then, months later when I was interviewing with Pfizer for a sales job, he told me I was "an idiot" if I didn't take the job. Tired of having my intelligence questioned, I looked no further and accepted Pfizer's offer.

Three years later, I got promoted into the new Urology division built around a soon-to-be-launched erection pill. When Vitamin V became a media and social sensation, I knew I had the hook for the book I always wanted to write.

Ten years after Dad called me "an idiot," I got published. Universal paid me a lot of money for the movie rights.

- Jamie Reidy, Author of *Hard Sell: The Evolution of a Viagra Salesman*

When I was just out of college, I got a job at a fortune 500 company. After two years, I realized that I just wasn't interested in what I was doing. I called my Dad, whining about how boring my job was and he told me that it is up to me to make my career interesting. He told me that only I can help myself and that since I was young and unattached it was time to shake things up and take some risks. I did just that by quitting my job and traveling around Europe for three months. It was that trip that helped me get my head together and find a new path.

- Meagan Farrell, Clear the Clutter,
www.cleartheclutterprofessionalorganizing.blogspot.com

I've wanted to own my own business for about as long as I can remember (I even subscribed to Inc. magazine in high school). After college I started exploring entrepreneurial opportunities. Dad, a successful litigation attorney, recommended that I figure out what I thought I wanted to do and then first work FOR a large company in the same industry and/or a similar company in a different market. He told me I'd learn what they did that worked and, just as importantly, what they did that did not. So true. I worked in and around the IT industry in small, mid-size and Fortune 500 companies for ten years. I saw the good, the bad, and what was missing. Now I own a successful business that fills an under served niche. Thanks, Dad!

- Jennifer Whitlock, Principle, www.thehelpdeskcompany.com

When I was about 25, my Dad, who was an executive with General Electric for many years, saw the end of the white collar career path and he said to me: "Kim, you have to work for yourself."

Well, he was right. And while it took me another 10 years to branch out on my own, I started a public relations business and have never looked back. I love NOT WORKING for people, except the people I want to have as clients. But I have purposely not grown or expanded, more than a one person office with 5-6 subcontractors. I have brought some of my favorite workers on full time at the companies I consult with, so that the employees can have benefits and stability, but I didn't want that for myself.

I have insurance, 401K and all the benefits that anyone else has, just not the BS of WORKING FOR SOMEONE.

My dad, saw something in me that I didn't even see in myself and it was the best advice that I ever took from him, oh, other than invest all that was possible in my Government Thrift savings plan, that is HUGE now, seeing I contributed from age 22-27!!

- Kim Fuller, Kim Fuller Public Affairs, Tulsa

My father was the head partner of a Wall St. law firm. He always told me: "You are a professional. There is no one at work who you should not call by their first name."

Over the years, that served me extremely well. It avoided creating an artificial barrier with senior executives that would stand in the way of building rapport and creating impactful relationships.

- John West Hadley, Career Search Counselor, www.jhacareers.com

As the middle of three daughters, my sisters and I always are receiving advice from my dad, Steve Hagendorf, a retired municipal bond salesman and current volunteer children's story-hour reader.

"If you don't ask, you don't get. The worst they can say is no."

"If you have to choose between a pay-raise and a title change, take the money. You can't pay your bills with a fancy business card."

"If you always do what you always have done, you only can get what you already have."

- Lisa Hagendorf, Director of PR, Digital Media, www.playboy.com

Growing up with an entrepreneurial dad gave me a lot of exposure to the working world at a very early age. I had my first 'office job' working in the accounting department of his engineering firm at age 13. It was an extremely boring, tedious position that involved me filing and putting reinforcement tabs on three-ring binder holes of accounting ledgers. (Gosh, do I really need to be admitting that I was working in a time when there weren't computers?) I remember telling my dad after about a week into my new job that if this was what having a career was like, then I didn't want to grow up. He laughed and said the following phrase to me:

How far you go in your career will depend on how much !@#$ you are willing to put up with.

I heard this phrase from him more than once in my lifetime, and each time he said it, he always followed up by showing me how to look at the work I was doing as part of the bigger picture (ie. how it would build my skills, open doors of opportunity, be valued by others, etc.). In short, he reminded me that how I chose to look at the work I was doing was exactly that – my choice. This is so true! You can look at work as a personal sacrifice, or an endless opportunity to experience, learn and grow. When you do the latter, success seems to materialize. It's the attitude that makes the difference in the outcome.

- J.T. O'Donnell, Author of *Careerealism*, www.jtodonnell.com

A dedicated musician from the age of ten, with aspirations of becoming a rock star by the age of 15, Dad's advice was as simple as "be sure to have a day job to fall back on in case the music aspirations don't pan out." Because, he would say, "'Luck' is defined as when opportunity and preparedness meet and if you don't have the most basic of business experience and skills to recognize 'Luck' when you see it, you will miss out on a great many opportunities in life."

While living in New York City during the 1980's, pursuing a career as a hard rock guitarist through and after college, I continued working in full time day jobs that provided me with a tremendous amount of real world experience in sales, marketing, advertising and public relations. I was always naturally gifted at selling and promoting, so I soaked up these business skills like a sponge. They quickly crossed over to my musical passions and I always became the de facto manager, publicist and marketer for the majority of the bands I performed in.

My passion and knowledge of the music industry, combined with these business skills, paid off in spades in the early 1990's, when I was in my late 20's, when I aggressively sought out and scored the position of sales and marketing manager with a leading importer and distributor of musical instruments.

Quickly realizing I was a far better marketer and promoter than musician, I gave up my aspirations at becoming a professional musician and immersed myself into my new career with this company. Almost instantly, I began working with some of the biggest recording artists in the world, including band members for Madonna, Michael Jackson, Stevie Wonder and Whitney Houston, to name just a few. My career in the music industry was underway.

By early 1994, I relocated from my hometown in the Metro New York-area to Northern California where I founded my music and entertainment publicity agency, PRThatRocks.com, which continues to work with the biggest manufacturers of musical instruments, major label bands, legendary recording studios, concert tours and events - including promoting Playboy Mansion events - as well as entertainment industry philanthropic organizations.

In July 2007, PRThatRocks.com was featured in PRWeek Magazine, the publicity industry's leading trade publication, for its innovative campaign strategies. I, along with my client, Singer/songwriter Melanie Dekker, were nominated for two 2008 Los Angeles Music Awards, for Independent Music Video of the Year and the National Community Service Award of the Year.

My father, born in 1924, a product of the Great Depression, and a veteran of World War II, held the same job all of his life, provided a great upbringing and home for my mother, brother and I, but never pursued his true dreams, nor did he ever reveal any the way I did. He was also never the kind of guy that would tell me he was proud of me by making my dreams a reality, but his friends would always tell me he would constantly rave about my exploits backstage at the Grammy Awards, rock concerts, etc., and that he was very proud I actually "figured out a way to get paid for all that playing around."

- Christopher Buttner, President, www.prthatrocks.com

When I was in high school, my best friend's dad refused to let him quit his job as a supermarket bag boy. He said that it wouldn't look good on his son's resume for him to have quit a job after only 6 months.

He made a huge deal out of it, like being a bag boy in the supermarket was really paving the way for his future. He stayed in the bag boy job, lasted one year in college, and now drives a delivery truck for a living. Those months bagging groceries obviously served him well!

- Candice Broom, www.mommosttraveled.com

My father kept telling me to be an accountant. I was a psych major until the second semester of my senior year. I had to change majors to writing because I couldn't pass the required statistics course. Who ever heard of a dyslexic accountant? Unless that's what Wall Street is full of and why we're in the mess we are.

I eventually got an MFA in Creative Writing and teach English as a Foreign Language overseas. I'm smart enough numbers-wise to know teaching overseas means no income taxes in the USA (teachers don't make anything near the taxable $80,000 a year).

- A. Delaney Walker

Said to me by my dad when I was the CEO of my own 10-person new media agency in NYC:

Dad: "Why don't you get a job as a secretary at (specific company) in NJ? You can get health benefits and a 401K!"

Me: "Um, Dad, I am the CEO of my own successful company, and I offer my employees health benefits and a 401K."

I guess the idea of the supposed "security" of having a meager-paying, but health-benefit offering secretarial job trumped the independence and unlimited potential of heading one's own company. I laughed off the advice my dad gave me and have started 3 more companies since.

- Christine Harmel, Interactive Resource, www.interactiveresource.com

My dad once told me this: "Someone always gets drunk and acts like a fool at the office christmas party ... don't let it be you!" He also said: "Be the first one there and the last one to leave. "

- **Jan Luongo, APR, Alliance Communications, Inc.**

I thought I could share these two snippets of advice from my father, who is in a blue collar small business profession, didn't go to University because the school system, did not realize he is dyslexic (something I figured out when in high school) though he is more than intelligent enough.

Best: When I was in high school, Dad gave me the best advice to 'always carry a notebook and pencil, take notes everywhere, so nobody can ask you what you are doing' – fast forward 20 years later, in my career I have learned to listen and take notes so well, that our companies' clients appreciate it and see it as a differentiation of our service.

Worst: "Stay at safe big company job." – Instead of ditching to co-found a software and consultancy company (in my case Royal Dutch Shell (Oil)), "because the neighbor who worked there who lives up the road, has a good pension from them." After 35 years of service – which is longer than I have been alive, and cannot conceive of staying in bureaucracy for that long.

- **Naomi F. Moneypenny, VP Research & Technology, ManyWorlds Inc., www.manyworlds.com**

I spent my 20's teaching and working with schizophrenic and emotionally disturbed children. I knew by the time I met my wife-to-be that I couldn't make a living that way any longer, so...I talked it over with my Dad. He told me, "Con, if you are a bird made for bigger flight, it takes a while to spread your wings. Keep following the wind and enjoy the adventure. You'll find your way."

He was right, of course. Because this was the advice he always lived and the way he always believed, I grew up to follow that creed. Opportunity knocked - programming calling! - and I made what some would see as an improbable leap and spread my wings. It has led to great career success in a field made for this perspective, the computing field. Yet, it was the "wing spreading" period for me that keeps life's connections from being sterile or hollow, always endowing the adventure with human meaning.

…And the winds carried me right to Silicon Valley, don't ya know! Even though my Mom would love us back in small town Kansas.

- **Conrad Hake, Conolay Consulting, Inc., San Francisco**

My father told me to find a career to fall back on so that I can help my husband if needed after all the husband supports the family and I won't have to work all my life.. oops.. that didn't happen. While I started off in education I have had several different careers and after I got divorced started my own business; that was 13 years ago. My father also told me that women are the supportive role to enable the men to run the companies. Talk about old school.

- **Harriet Cohen, Training Solutions**

1. Get a degree in Business because it will serve you well
2. Pick a nice place to live and then find a job there
3. Work in an area of your interest/strength (in this case, my son loves sports so he works for FieldTur)
4. If you want freedom and opportunity to make money, learn how to sell
5. If you can sell, you will never be out of work, and if by chance you are, you won't be for long.

- **Ken Keller, Renaissance Executive Forums, www.invest-5-hours.com**

"If you're thinking about changing jobs, the last person with whom you should consult is someone who loves you." – They'll want to hold you tight and protect you from any risk.

"A gut instinct is not a good economic indicator."

- **Hilary Chalmers, www.foodjobsbook.com**

During my freshman year of college, I went in to see an academic advisor to figure out what my major should be. I told her that I was thinking about getting a business degree because it would enable me to graduate and get a good paying job. She asked me if I enjoyed business and I told her that I didn't. She asked me what I was good at and I explained that I liked writing and creativity.

She suggested that I get an English degree. I told her that I wouldn't be able to get a good job with that degree and she explained that making bad grades in a business degree would probably harm me more than making good grades in an English degree. She said simply "Do what you're good at, and you will be successful." I've taken her advice many times since then and now have a successful hypnotherapy business. Looking back, I probably wouldn't have thought that I would be able to make money doing this either, but although it is unconventional, I'm good at it and that has really worked for me.

- **Laura Ryan-Day, A New Day Hypnosis, www.anewdayhypnosis.com**

The best advice I ever received in business was from my father. One day I asked him what something was worth and he said "Something is only worth what someone will pay for it." He went on to explain that you can have land that is valued at $100,000, but if someone is only willing to give you $10 for it, well that is what it is worth. In this economy that really hits home.

- Sasha Windes, www.freshandgreen.com

Commercial airline pilot and father of five children, my dad, Mike Banker, put all of us kids through college. Thanks to mom and dad and all of his sage advice. Now, he's got five grown kids with careers as: Electrical Engineer, Doctor, PR/Marketing (me), Lawyer, Pilot. Thanks dad, nice work!

"It's easiest to find a job when you already have one." – Meaning ANY job is better while you find THE perfect job!

"Half of the battle is just showing up on time, every day." – Be on time, stay until 5 – and you are half way there. You'd be amazed at how many people CAN'T do this.

"Try it, you might like it." – Who knows, you might be passing up something you actually enjoy.

- Christine Fanning, Schiedermayer & Associates, www.schied.com

My dad has always been a hard worker, he came to this country from Chile in the '70's, alone and with no family here. Did not know the language or what he would find here. He started at the bottom and worked his way up. He was a bus boy for a while holding multiple jobs for a few restaurants and eventually began to learn how to cook. He has been a cook ever since and long before I was born and one of the best at every restaurant he worked. Heard of The Hilltop Steakhouse in Saugus, MA? It was quite famous back in the day. He was the number 1 broiler man, king of the steaks.

His advice to his 3 kids had always been to work hard, be on-time and always want to learn. A saying he still tells me to this day "Find the best in the place, learn from them, then beat them." Once you have beat the best, you have accomplished all you can there. You are valued and important.

The downside though to that is, you have to realize when you are getting taken advantage of and being abused at work once you are the best. If you are no longer getting the help you need to do a good job because you have been able to handle a great deal on your own, you need to make that known. So the lesson overall from my father is to strive to be the best wherever you go but realize there is a downside to being the best and don't get taken advantage of.

- Karina Manriquez, Recruiting Specialist, www.resourcefulrecruiting.com

The most interesting thing my Dad shared with me was more recent. He said that it's nice for a husband and wife to balance careers – one in public service for the long-term security/benefits/pension, and the other in the private sector for financial success/opportunity. I thought it was an interesting perspective.

- Kathy De Santi

When I first told my dad that I wanted to be a photographer, he thought I wanted to open a retail photography store and sell cameras and film supplies being a business man himself. When I explained that I wanted to do portraits of people, he became my best salesman by writing to all the ceo's of his stock holdings explaining that his daughter was a portrait photographer. He taught me the importance of pursuing my career with unrelenting persistence.

- Nancy Rica Schiff, Photographer, Author, *Odd Jobs, Portraits of Unusual Occupations*, and *Odder Jobs, More Portraits of Unusual Occupations*, www.nancyricaschiff.com

My late father Harry Falkenthal advised me over and over that I should become a dentist. He felt it was the best possible career because you were a medical professional and could call yourself "Doctor," but the hours were great and you were not on call around the clock like an OB/GYN or ER physician. You could run your own office as a small businessperson. It wasn't too bloody or gross. And you made a lot of money for the time worked!

I would roll my eyes and say, "Well Dad, go right ahead and go to dental school!" He wasn't a dentist – he ran a motorcycle parts and service shop and did custom work, a craftsman and blue collar entrepreneur. How he came to this conclusion, I have no idea.

No, I didn't become a dentist – I got my bachelor's degree in radio-television and my master's degree in mass communication. I was a broadcast journalist and producer for 15 years, and I've now been a public relations professional for 15 years. But I never had any doubt my father was proud of my educational and career accomplishments. What Dad never realized is that the lively conversations about current events, books, political science, history, and just about everything else in our household from the time I could talk was the best possible preparation I could have gotten for a career in communications.

Unfortunately Dad died at age 55 in 1993 so he didn't live to see me start my business. He would have been delighted that at least one of his children inherited his entrepreneurial gene. FYI, his advice didn't work with my brother or sister either – my brother is a computer engineer and my sister is an attorney.

- Gayle Lynn Falkenthal, APR, Falcon Valley Group, San Diego

Here are a few things my dad said that make great job advice:

"Shut up and listen."

"The boss is always a son-of-a-bitch."

"There's no easy way to make a fast buck. If it looks too good to be true, it is."

"It is called 'work' for a reason."

- Tracy Bagatelle-Black, www.bagatelleblack.com

My dad starts every conversation off with "What you need to do…"

My dad is from the 'good ol' boy' network and taught us kids to do the same. He 'forced' me into a sorority to 'get a good job.' Later in life, I tried to use my 'connections' to land a great job at a major commercial real estate firm – two of my friends were already there. The HR director was sorority alumnae from a different university. After the secret handshake (kidding) and reminiscing about college days, I felt like the job was in the bag - Dad was right! She checked not only my stellar business references, but also my sorority 'references.' She learned that I had almost gotten kicked out of the sorority for various incidents and I did not get the job. The HR director sent me a letter stating that I was not the 'right fit' for their organization.

My dad said 'what you need to do…is start behaving yourself.' Of course, it was the best thing to have happened…I'm an entrepreneur and very happy to behave however I like.

- Susie Shina, Fitness Lifestylist, Author, Speaker & Fit Enough Entrepreneur, www.susieshina.com

My dad taught me one of the most important lessons in my working life. Way back when, I had my first job working in our local grocery store. It was long hours (8:30 pm – 6 pm) and five or six days a week during the summer. You were on your feet all day ringing the cash register (and actually counting change) or stocking shelves. When you're seventeen, that seems like hard work.

One Saturday, our busiest day, I had been out too late the night before. I felt so tired I came home from work. I then recovered and decided I was well enough to go to the beach with my friends. My dad thought otherwise. He told me to get back in the car and drove me back to work. The value of both going to work and doing your job well were a lesson I learned well from my father. He, by the way, never took one sick day, ever, in all the many years he worked.

- Alison Doyle, About.com Job Search Guide and About.com Guide to Job Security, www.about.com

CH 6: BEST AND WORST CAREER ADVICE FROM OTHER DADS

The top advice my dad always told me was to show up to work early, especially in the beginning when you start your job. He always said that showing up to work earlier than you had to always showed a great impression with your boss, and he was right.

When I worked at a PR firm in South Carolina, I used to show up about 30 minutes early. The husband of the CEO was the CFO, and he and I used to talk about sports and other news of the day. He and the CEO knew that I traveled to work from about 25 miles away. There were some days that there was a major accident, and I was going to run late, and I called and they understood. I was never questioned if I was running late to work because they knew that I had a good reason to be late. Needless to say, they were very impressed that I would show up to work earlier than I had to.

He also told me that when you are working for a good company that sometimes you would have to make sacrifices, but in the end it would pay off. My dad worked for one company for 30 years, and he mentions this one story about giving up something that paid off.

In the early 80's, my dad's company had a major project that had come up, and his company asked a for a volunteer to help out on this major project, and someone had to sacrifice their weekend. My dad stepped up and offered to help, even though he had a family vacation planned in the mountains. The company knew that, but he insisted that he could go another weekend and he would be willing to help on this project. My dad worked on the project, and everything turned out very well.

In the late 80's my mom got sick with cancer, and he approached his company and told them about what was happening. They told him that he could take as much time off as he needed and to let them know when and how long and they would work it out. They were very accommodating with my dad during the 20 months my mom was sick before she passed away. He always told us that the company never forgot that he sacrificed his vacation time for that project, and they repaid him during this time and the rest of the time he was with the company. He always has told all of us to step up with there is a major project and volunteer because the big bosses will remember these things.

I definitely have listened to him! In my current job, there have been a couple of instances where there was something going on at work, and I offered to come in early to help. I never complained, and I showed up to do my job. The executive director definitely notices this and all of my hard work, and I have received gift certificate and recognition for it. I remember in the back of my mind what my father always tells me, and I know that in the end it will pay off!

**- Sabrina Kidwai, Media Relations Manager,
Association for Career & Technical Education**

I love my Dad, but I once told him I wanted to be a teacher like him, and he looked me right in the eye and said "Oh, another failure." Most of the time he jokes around but he wasn't kidding. So either consciously or subconsciously, I've tried to avoid teaching jobs.

- **Brandon J. Mendelson, Published American Humorist**

My beloved dad (Otto F. Thaler, MD) once told me not to make any drastic changes until you've been in a new job for at least six weeks, unless making immediate changes is why you've been hired. It takes awhile to get the hang of the personalities, processes/systems, and needs. Creating change too quickly comes across as unnecessarily aggressive and over-confident, which creates bad feelings among co-workers and can poison the workplace permanently.

- **Ruth E. Thaler-Carter, Freelance Writer/Editor, www.writerruth.com**

When I was in my early 20's and just starting my own marketing consulting business, my Dad sent me a note with this advice:

"You don't get what you deserve, you get what you negotiate." I have always tried to keep this in mind when I was negotiating contracts with clients.

- **Heidi Niehart, Marketing Consultant/Creator&Co-Producer of Tot-a-Doodle-Do! Children's DVDs & Craft Kits, San Diego**

My dad has always given me great advice about career moves. Some of his best words of wisdom were:

"If you make a mistake, admit it. Don't cover it up. Don't lie. Don't blame it on Susie or Bobby (even if they were partially to blame). Immediately tell your boss that you made a mistake, and then follow up with how you are going to fix it. It is better to be honest and show your ability to be proactive then being caught in a lie."

"Never, ever, ever go in to an interview (or salary negotiation, etc.) thinking about what the company can do for you. Put yourself in the place of the interviewer. No one wants an employee who wants to take, take, take. If you think about what you can do for the company and how you can benefit them, they will be much more receptive to you."

"Keep track of your accomplishments. Document them. Make copies of great presentations; take photos if you pull off a great event, keep copies of thank you notes and emails, etc. You never know when you might need to reinforce a skill set you have to a potential employer."

- **Lindsay Anvik, Recruitment Consultant, RJL Resources, Inc, www.rjlresources.com**

Advice from my dad: The best reason not to lie is that you have to have an amazing memory to remember what you said if you don't tell the truth.

Advice from me (I'm in my mid 70's): Make up a different resume for each job you are applying for. Do not lie or exaggerate on your resume but rather enlarge the description of the experience you have that matches the position and cut back the description on area of experience that are not a match.

Most importantly make sure the summary of experience at the top is written as closely as possible to provide the "right" information to attract the attention of the recruiter who is reading it as this summary usually results in your resume being read in full or put aside.

If you have not interviewed for a job in a long time, apply for a position you are not interested in as a "practice interview". It is a great learning experience. You don't want to have your first interview with the employer that you most want to work for.

- Arthur Koff, Author, *Invent Your Retirement*, Retired Brains, www.retiredbrains.com

Growing up I always knew I'd be a journalist. I went to school at Newhouse, Syracuse University. When I graduated, I went looking for a job in Manhattan and had a lot of "no's." I got really discouraged and my dad said, "Keep going, it'll come." I finally wound up taking a job at a tiny publishing company as a receptionist for $18K. It was so upsetting to graduate with this magazine editing & writing/marketing degree and be…meaningless.

I was in that position for 8 months total, when the publisher's parent company stole me away. I became the associate editor of Teen Beat magazine – every 22-year-old's dream job. I made a bit more money but began thriving in my position.

I'd tell my dad everything – I loved the job and was good at it, but there was no money, and he'd say, "If you do what you love, the money will come. Well, he was right. I kept plugging and began getting noticed in the publishing world. I made it to editor-in-chief before I moved to Florida.

In Florida, I became editor of BIZBASH FLORIDA, which made me fall in love with Special Events. I now own a communications company, and make more money than I ever thought I would, working in an industry I am crazy about. Granted, it took 20 years to get here, but my dad's advice was sound.

If you do what you love, the rest will come!

- Shari Lynn Rothstein-Kramer, SLK Creative, www.slkcreative.com

I grew up in a home with a father who was a Physical Fitness professor and speaker, basketball official, marathon runner, outdoorsman and landowner who capitalized on every inch of his terrain to support his family. My dad instilled in me at a very young age the ultimate value of healthy living, taking care of what you own, and not being afraid to dirty and work hard for your income. As he so eloquently would put it, "Don't drag your a - -. The light ain't gonna get any greener." Meaning, no one is going to do it for you, so put your head down and go! Underneath that all, though was the foundational lesson that being disciplined is one of the best values I could ever have. Not surprisingly, the renowned words of Coach Mike Krzyzewski could have just as easily come direct from my Pop: "Discipline is doing what you are supposed to do in the best possible manner the time you are supposed to do it. And that's not such a bad thing." Trust me, it is ingrained in my noggin. Just ask me how 3000 hand-planted Christmas tree samplings can yield 4 years of college tuition!

That said, being a headstrong, curious Aries, just like my pop, he and I used to but heads all the time while I was growing up. And a little mantra was born: I don't know enough to not ask or not try. Because of this early-born drive, I would create friction and make a mess everywhere I went, trying to figure things out, getting into situations where "a talking to" was inevitable. Alas, the proverbial "wait 'til your father gets home" was a familiar tough-love statement in the Dykeman household…always aimed at Kimmie. But as I grew up, and eventually became "my own boss" after college, I earned the freedom to travel anywhere in the world and courageously explore any avenues of work, play, and adventure. My Dad's "parenting" certainly diminished , but his guidance, priceless values and support for my independent nature have remained timeless and timely impressions in my life.

No, I didn't become a teacher…and I still have no spouse, no house, no dog to call my own. But my love affairs with entrepreneurialism, Mother Nature and the great outdoors most certainly bloomed from his influence to create a life full of passion, joy, wild successes, and unpredictable experiences. The apple doesn't fall far from the tree, and just like Pop, my mission to motivate, entertain and educate folks to live life to its fullest is the one love that gets me out of bed each day. Ask anyone to describe Kimberlie Dykeman, and they'll be sure to list at the top: courageous…and the most disciplined and hardest working person they know. To Richard Dykeman, I owe the credit!

- Kimberlie Dykeman, www.puresoapbox.com

While my dad was never a career strategist and never even had to face a career transition (he was with one company for 30 years), he did give me some sage advice about my career along the way. Here are a few of my favorite nuggets:

A lot of bosses are idiots. Everyone I've ever met has an interesting story about a bad boss. The trick is to figure out either how to manage that relationship or get out of it. The DISC assessment tool is very useful for figuring out how you communicate with people and how those around you respond to your method of communication. It can help you discover how to tweak your communication style to improve your relationship with a difficult boss.

You will never be able to please everyone. It seems like our entire lives are spent trying to please someone…a teacher, a boss, a family member. Some people only hear from their bosses when something goes wrong. Be sure to keep track of your stories of success throughout the year so your discussion at performance review time focuses on your positive contributions rather than just the things that need to be improved.

No job is worth risking your health for. I meet many people who have sacrificed their health for their jobs. Stress can contribute to numerous health issues including obesity, heart disease, and depression. Examine your career choices and regularly assess how well they are aligned with your overall life goals.

Getting fired is not the worst thing that can happen in life. Being fired can be an enormous blow to one's ego, but many people report that it was the best thing that ever happened to them because it allowed them to gain perspective on a bad situation, discover their strengths, and move forward to a more fulfilling career.

Put as much money in your 401k as you can. These plans are an easy, relatively painless way to save money. There's really no reason for anyone, even someone who is just starting out in their career, to pass up this opportunity.

Don't expect others to manage your career. My dad taught me a long time ago that no one cares about my career as much as I do. It's certainly beneficial to have a mentor along the way, but ultimately you have to own your career. Take responsibility for that ownership by keeping your resume up to date, networking regularly, maintaining relationships with recruiters, and monitoring your online identity.

- Barbara Safani, Author of *Happy About My Resume*, www.careersolvers.com

My dad was very advanced in his thinking. I went to school in the 60's and, coming up through the language side of things, my mother wanted me to study Greek and German (I was already studying French, Spanish and Latin). NO, said my father, she takes TYPING. He already knew computers were going to be the way of the world – his office had one of the first computers around, and he said that if I didn't know how to type (keyboard) I would be UNEMPLOYABLE.

As a result of Dad's advice, I typed my way through university, charging other students to type their essays. I was one of the first people in my office to get and use a computer because of my typing skills and, today, thanks to Dad's advice, I am connected. I type over 100 words per minute with a high degree of accuracy; I take all my client's notes on computer while they are talking to me because my first job was a dicta-typist.

Where would I be if he hadn't intervened? Probably wondering exactly how I was going to keep my Greek fresh! Thanks, Dad.

- **Angela Sutcliffe, Sutcliffe Consulting, www.angelasutcliffe.com**

About The Author

G.L. Hoffman is a serial entrepreneur and venture investor/operator/incubator/mentor. Two of his companies have traveled the entire success path from the garage to IPO. He has been featured in Forbes, Wall Street Journal and other local business publications and newspapers.

Currently, he is Chairman of JobDig, an employment-focused media company that delivers multi-channel recruitment advertising solutions to employers of all sizes in all industries. JobDig publishes a free weekly jobs newspaper in markets throughout the U.S., operates the popular website jobDig.com, and partners with network and cable TV stations and radio stations in each of its markets to allow companies to leverage broadcast media in their recruitment advertising. The company also owns and operates LinkUp.com, a site that aggregates and publishes only jobs listed on corporate web sites from over 10,000 companies around the U.S.

His daily blog can be found at www.whatwoulddadsay.com, jobdig.com, and now as a weekly guest writer at US News and World Report.

www.ingramcontent.com/pod-product-compliance
Ingram Content Group UK Ltd.
Pitfield, Milton Keynes, MK11 3LW, UK
UKHW022231230426
12048UKWH00016BA/1199